CONTENTS

Contents

This page has been left blank for double-sided copying.

TABLES

This page has been left blank for double-sided copying.

EXECUTIVE SUMMARY

As the largest of the 15 food and nutrition assistance programs administered by the U.S. Department of Agriculture (USDA), the Supplemental Nutrition Assistance Program (SNAP) is a central component of our nation's nutrition assistance safety net. SNAP provides nutrition assistance benefits and nutrition education services to low-income individuals and families in an effort to reduce hunger and improve the health and well-being of low-income people nationwide. While evaluation research has assessed whether the program is achieving these objectives, less is known about the challenges low-income families face and their coping strategies to remain food secure, defined as having adequate access to food for an active, healthy life.

This report presents findings from the qualitative In-Depth Interview component of the SNAP Food Security (SNAPFS) study. The main SNAPFS study was conducted for the Food and Nutrition Service of the USDA from October 2011 through September 2012, and examined the effects of the program on food security for 6,436 SNAP households just entering the program and 3,275 households on SNAP for approximately six to seven months. The in-depth interview effort discussed in this report was conducted between February 2012 and June 2012 and consisted of detailed qualitative discussions held with a small subset of 90 SNAP households with children in six states about their financial situations, their use of SNAP, and their overall food security. Interviews were held in the homes of the respondents, unless they preferred to meet in a public location like a library or coffee shop. Interview questions focused on expenditures and income, SNAP and food shopping habits, eating habits, nutrition, triggers of food hardship, and food-related coping strategies. The purpose of this formative, qualitative study was to provide important insights into the challenges low-income families face and their coping strategies to purchase all of the food that they need in the face of a shortfall in resources, and to inform the direction of future research on food security, including hypothesis generation and instrument design.

This analysis was descriptive; however, for each theme, we systematically assessed whether there were especially large differences in general financial circumstances, food hardships and coping strategies, eating and food dynamics, and in the role SNAP plays in meeting a family's nutritional needs by food security level and by race/ethnicity. We observed several of the former but almost no meaningful differences among the latter. As qualitative works which involve similar types of analysis have noted, a small qualitative study cannot make causal claims; therefore, the analysis in this study should be read as helpful descriptions to guide the formation of hypotheses about the mechanisms and processes that might underlie variations in food security, and the role of the SNAP program.

FINDINGS

General Financial Circumstances and the Role of SNAP in Beneficiaries' Finances

The fundamental reality of most SNAP recipients' lives is that expenses often outstrip income. SNAP households experience both recurring and episodic financial strain that is eased but not alleviated in full by participation in the SNAP program. SNAP allows families to set aside more easily a portion of their resources—SNAP—for food, and to prioritize a healthier, more consistent diet without compromising as much on obligations such as rent, utilities, transportation, and other basic needs. Families in this study often build their monthly budgets around SNAP, allocating their fungible cash resources toward their bills and other, often urgent, financial needs triggered by a sudden loss of income or increase in expenditure. SNAP eases the financial tradeoffs families must make as they strive to bring their budgets into balance, and may stave off material hardship in a variety of domains. Nonetheless, the families in this study do frequently run short of the financial resources necessary to purchase all of the food that they need. We show that though many recipients experience these shortfalls routinely—as often as the end of every month—few earmark additional cash resources for food. These resources are often fully allocated to other purposes. However, households who run out of food benefits toward the end of the month frequently find ways of allocating some additional cash for food even though it may not have been earmarked earlier.

Financial struggle often occurs despite access to the social safety net, as well as the significant efforts families make at belt tightening: keeping the lights off to lower the utility bill, or even forgoing a trip to church to save on fuel. It also occurs despite the fact that families often "juggle": they pay some of their bills while negotiating with or even defaulting on other creditors. These practices, besides incurring late fees and reconnection charges, put many households in serious debt—debt that constrains future access to credit. Other strategies include doubling up with relatives, gleaning other kinds of network support, running up credit cards, and bringing in small amounts of extra cash via entrepreneurial activities such as braiding hair or selling tin cans or plasma. However, these ways of dealing with overburdened monthly budgets have sharp limitations and are not equally available to all.

Differences Among the Food Secure and Food Insecure Related to Food Hardships and Coping Strategies

Financial Shortfalls and Food Security

A household is "food secure" if it has access at all times to enough food for an active, healthy life for all its members and "food insecure" if it has difficulty getting enough food because of a lack of resources. Households that experienced particularly severe levels of food insecurity are designated as having "very low food security." Similarly, in this report, the term "financial shortfall" is used to mean a situation where a family is unable to pay one or more of its non-food bills for a month or more.

The families interviewed in our study typically manage their food budgets with great care, but small changes in income or expenditures can result in an episode of food hardship. A job loss, the birth of a child, a medical emergency or expensive prescription, or the high cost of gasoline can precipitate an unstable situation in which families must make sacrifices to maintain their food security. We found the following triggers of financial shortfall, in order of frequency: (1) temporal variation in resources or expenses; (2) unusually high recurring expenses, (3) unexpected and sudden financial shocks in income or expenditure, and (4) loss or reduction in benefits from government programs.

As would be expected, there are strong associations between the financial shortfalls we document with regard to food and the level of food security a household was experiencing at the time of the survey. We found that the less food secure the household is, the more likely it is that a household has experienced a financial shortfall due to an abrupt loss of income or a sudden increase in expenses. Also, households with very low food security are more likely to report a financial shortfall due to high recurring expenses such as prescription drugs or, for those with a considerable commute to work, gasoline for the car. Finally, we note what appears to be a strong relationship between experiencing a financial shortfall due to a disruption in government benefits and household food security status as measured by the quantitative SNAPFS survey. Most typically, this relates to the loss of or reduction in SNAP benefits due to changes in income or failure to comply with program recertification requirements or administrative error. Notably, no household in the food secure group reported that an unexpected drop in government benefits triggered a spell of financial hardship.

Food Coping Strategies and Food Security

We found that respondents employed coping strategies that are both reactive—to deal with food hardship—and proactive—to avoid it. The latter type include (1) restricting food intake; (2) altering the kinds of foods consumed; (3) turning to networks; (4) visiting food pantries; and (5) scouring the ads for sales, traveling from store to store several times a month to ensure the best bargains, and planning meals almost entirely around the sales.

We also noted differences in coping strategies used across food security levels. The least food secure were considerably more likely to say they had to restrict food intake—skip meals—to cope with a shortfall than those who were more food secure. This is not surprising, as the definition of food security takes skipping meals into account. Note, however that there were a number of food secure households who report routinely skipping meals; they do so with such regularity that it is considered routine and may thus be under-reported. There was also a notable relationship between a household's food security status and whether it changed the type of food it consumed toward the end of the month to cope with a shortfall, such as by shifting from meat to ramen noodles.

Another coping strategy that differed by food security status was related to family networks. We found that a significant minority of the food secure households take advantage of frequent invitations to relatives' homes for meals and receive contributions of groceries and cash from their family and friends. These households can usually rely on their networks to provide cash, groceries, or meals when SNAP benefits run out toward the end of the month. Those who are less food secure have less access to such resources. In fact, households with very low food security often explicitly state they do not have networks that are able or willing to provide. And even those in this group who do often cannot rely on them, usually because the donor is in a financial situation similar to their own. Those who shared their SNAP with others not in the official SNAP household were also clustered in the very low food security group, suggesting that when respondents extend charity to the even less fortunate, it is costly to their own well-being.

Finally, those households who are the least food secure are also the least likely to engage in a key form of proactive coping. This strategy involves carefully researching the best prices on particular products, traveling to multiple grocery stores—sometimes a considerable distance away—several times a month to capitalize fully on sales, and carefully planning the meals around what is on sale rather than on the households' food preferences. Managing one's food budget in this way requires considerable skill, and this skill is often richly evident in the narratives of the food secure.

Strategies Households Use to Meet Food Needs

SNAP recipients are usually strategic in trying to stretch their SNAP benefits out over the course of the month. Yet most households also reported that they compromised nutrition and variety in their diets to ensure that they could provide enough food for the least expense. Though most families are conscientious in trying to provide a balanced meal every day for dinner, nearly all emphasize that they would shop differently—buying fresh vegetables instead of frozen, or leaner cuts of meat or fish—if their food budgets permitted. To ensure that their food budget stretches, many households clip coupons and compare prices across stores, but some are particularly adept at shopping avidly for bargains, shopping often and at several different stores to capitalize on sales, and carefully planning their menus around items that are on sale rather than on what the family would prefer to eat. However, few among those lowest in food security are able to employ these more elaborate strategies, in part because their overall circumstances are less stable (more have had to double up and more have experienced a recent financial shock, for example).

Many of the especially savvy shoppers are able to build reserves of cheap non-perishable foods for leaner financial times. These reserves are drawn upon at the end of the month, when SNAP benefits are often gone, at times of the year when expenses typically rise or revenues fall, and in the face of a financial shock. Despite numerous cost-cutting strategies, most families find that they must maintain a repetitive diet of lesser quality to keep their family fed throughout the month.

Eating and Food Dynamics within the Household

Respondents mostly eat simple meals for breakfast and lunch, favoring foods that are quick to prepare, especially pre-packaged "instant" items. Yet most respondents also express considerable awareness of, and concern over, the need to provide nutritious, balanced meals and focus on dinner to meet that need. Most say they cannot afford to consume the healthy diet they would wish to, but do adopt their cooking strategies to make the diet they can afford as healthy as possible. For example, a few bake rather than fry meat, and most make sure to serve vegetables—even if frozen or canned—with the evening meal, while also providing ample starches to ensure that no one goes to bed hungry. Many try to instill a habit of healthy eating in their children, and many parents report that they provide their children with all the fresh fruits and vegetables they can afford. Yet children often prefer food with little nutritional value, and parents sometimes "splurge" so they can buy their children an occasional "treat" such as ice cream. When families entertain—usually to celebrate a birthday—many report often saving for months to be able to afford any extra food expenditures such occasions require.

While parents strive to deploy their SNAP benefits to maintain consistent and nutritious meals for their children (and generally succeed), a striking number—nearly half—report restricting their own food intake to ensure their children have enough to eat throughout the month. This is especially likely for the least food secure but is also evident for a sizeable minority of the food secure. Skipping meals is frequent in this sample of SNAP participants, so much so that such sacrifices have become routine and are seldom defined as food hardship; many say that they intentionally skip meals to ensure they will have enough food to last through the month. Those with health problems within the household, such as diabetes or food allergies, are often unable to adjust their diets to avoid sacrifice, or to fully accommodate their illness.

Role of SNAP in Helping Households Meet Family Food Needs

For most households, the SNAP benefit is not meant to cover all a family's food needs in a given month, because the family is expected to buy some food from its own resources. Nevertheless, families often indicate that SNAP is a "lifesaver". It enables them to buy more and healthier food than they otherwise might by ensuring that a portion of their resources—the SNAP benefit—is devoted solely to food. It also helps parents ensure that their children seldom suffer food hardship, even if they themselves must go without. SNAP can also prevent hardship in other domains, as cash resources are often fully devoted to bills and other critical financial needs. When families lose SNAP—a more common occurrence among the less food secure—they often forgo paying bills (credit cards, the phone bill, the utilities, or even the rent) to ensure that their children can eat, but the food they consume during these times is less plentiful and less nutritious. Beneficiaries often complain that their SNAP is exhausted in two or three weeks; this is especially so for the least food secure, in part because they seldom employ the elaborate money-saving grocery shopping techniques that are evident for about a quarter of those in the other, more food secure, groups.

Interestingly, many households organize their budgets around the expectation that SNAP will suffice for the whole month. This expectation is seldom realized among any group, but is an expectation especially common among the very low food secure. Even though experience might indicate that they must also earmark a portion of their cash resources for food, they generally do not. But even if they desired to do so, frequent budget shortfalls and income shocks might make it exceedingly difficult, if not impossible, to earmark much cash for food needs, especially among the least food secure, for whom income shocks were most common.

Most families at all food security levels had to usually scramble to some degree to meet their food needs at the end of the month. For those with strong, generous networks—more common among the more food secure—the scramble was greatly eased. Because SNAP is often central to households' food planning, the loss of or a reduction in SNAP benefits, even for a brief period, can have a catastrophic impact on the family budget. Respondents often complain that even small changes in earnings can lead to destabilizing benefit reductions, and that a slight paperwork delay at the periodic renewal can result in the loss of SNAP for a month or more. The loss of other government benefits leads to financial shortfalls as well, but none plays as large of a role as SNAP.

Many respondents complained about what they perceive as caseworker error or administrative issues such as the long waits at the Public Assistance office when reapplication requires in-person visits that can take hours away from work and wages. Many say that these strains are intensified by the negative attitudes of SNAP caseworkers, whom beneficiaries commonly perceive to be apathetic toward their plight and rude in face-to-face interactions. These characterizations stand in strong contrast to WIC, which is perceived favorably. Most respondents reported not having received any nutrition education advice or instruction from the SNAP program. By contrast, clients who were in both SNAP and WIC often cited the nutrition education they had received from WIC as being very useful. Overall, many respondents expressed a need for additional nutrition education assistance in SNAP.

POTENTIAL DIRECTIONS FOR FUTURE RESEARCH

The study's findings suggest several directions for future research.

- Obtaining detailed information about fluctuations in household expenses and income. This would include seeking more detailed information about SNAP participants' expenditures and incomes just after entering SNAP and following them through the first few months. It would allow researchers and policymakers to understand how households reallocate scarce income resources once they receive SNAP benefits to meet obligations such as rent, utilities, transportation, and other basic needs.

- Exploring family networks as a food coping strategy. Obtaining more detailed information related to households' access to family networks and the role of family networks in alleviating food insecurity would offer a greater understanding of the availability of help from family, friends, and community members; the extent to which households use these resources; and how this use varies throughout the month.

- Food access and proactive coping strategies to maintain food security. More research is needed on how households make food purchase decisions and how this relates to food security. In particular, more information is needed about the extent to which the proactive coping strategies described in the in-depth interviews help to alleviate food insecurity.

- The relationship between physical and mental health in needing SNAP. The findings in the current study suggest that health issues, both mental and physical, may contribute substantially to patterns of SNAP use—both in determining patterns of entry and exit and also in altering the probability of long term dependency. However, more research is needed about the incidence of such health-related factors in the SNAP population.

- Planning for the end of the month, when SNAP benefits typically run out. The findings in this study suggest that many households fail to budget money with which to buy food after exhausting their SNAP benefits. More research is needed to determine whether this is an aspect of the program that is not communicated adequately to participants, and if so, how the program can change this disconnect between program users and design.

- WIC versus SNAP – What works best in one that could be applied to the other? Many of our respondents seemed to feel that WIC could serve as a "model" program and could potentially offer ideas for improving SNAP. Additional interviewing of households participating in both programs would be useful, in order to focus more directly on comparing them. Such detailed probing might also be able to shed additional light on reasons for various attitudes expressed and the degree to which those attitudes are experience-based.

Much of the research suggested above might reasonably consist of a combination of in-depth interviews to obtain input from SNAP recipients, together with standard survey methods to obtain data for related quantitative analyses. For example, for fluctuations in expenditures and income, SNAP participants might provide input about expenditures and income through in-depth interviews, but standard survey methods could be used to learn about the actual fluctuations in circumstances that occur over time. For the relationship between SNAP use and physical and mental health, research could potentially involve a combination of closed-ended survey methods to obtain detailed information about health histories over time and also in-depth interviewing to obtain information on how respondents believe that health factors have affected them and their participation in SNAP.

I. INTRODUCTION

The Supplemental Nutrition Assistance Program (SNAP), the largest of the 15 food and nutrition assistance programs administered by the U.S. Department of Agriculture (USDA), is a central component of our nation's nutrition assistance safety net. SNAP provides nutrition assistance benefits and some nutrition education services to low-income individuals and families in an effort to reduce hunger and improve the health and well-being of low-income people nationwide.

This current report examines the dynamics of the detailed mechanisms by which SNAP affects the food security of its recipients. USDA and other researchers have increasingly used food security status both as a measure to assess the incidence of nutrition issues in the general population and as an outcome measure in evaluating SNAP and other public food programs. A household is "food secure" if it has access at all times to enough food for an active, healthy life for all its members. A food *insecurity* definition applies when households have difficulty getting enough food because a lack of resources. Food security research has focused on prevalence of food insecurity, as in the volumes of "Household Food Security in the United States" reports published annually by the Economic Research Service, USDA (Coleman-Jensen et al. 2012). These studies describe the food security of the U.S. population for groups defined by household characteristics such as household size, presence of children, income, and race and ethnicity. Researchers have also used food security as an outcome measure to evaluate the effects of SNAP on food insecurity. Recent reviews of this literature can be found in Nord and Golla (2011); Ratcliffe and McKernan (2010); and Yen et al. (2008). Less is known, however, about the challenges low-income families face in maintaining food security, their coping strategies to remain food secure, and the role of SNAP in helping to meet family food needs.

Below, we present findings from the In-Depth Interview (IDI) component of the SNAP Food Security (SNAPFS) study, which was conducted by Mathematica Policy Research for the Food and Nutrition Service of the USDA from October 2011 through September 2012. The main effort of the SNAPFS study examines the association between SNAP and food security for SNAP households just entering the program and households enrolled in SNAP for approximately six to seven months via a series of quantitative telephone surveys of close to 10,000 households. This piece of that effort, conducted between February 2012 and June 2012, describes 90 in-depth qualitative discussions held with SNAP households with children in six states about their financial situations, their use of SNAP, and their overall food security. Interviews were held in the homes of the respondents, unless they preferred to meet in a public location like a library or coffee shop. Interview questions focused on expenditures and income, SNAP and food shopping habits, eating habits, nutrition, and triggers of food hardship and food-related coping strategies. The purpose of this formative, qualitative study was to provide important insights into the challenges low-income families face and the coping strategies developed and used in these households with the goal of maintaining their family's food security. Insights gained from this effort will help to inform the direction of future research on food security at the household level, aid in the generation of hypotheses, and help guide future research instrument design.

A. Design of the SNAPFS In- Depth Interview Survey

The sample of respondents for the SNAPFS IDI survey was drawn from the main sample used in the full SNAPFS telephone survey.[1] The telephone survey collected information from 9,811 SNAP households in 30 States from October 2011 through February 2012. This group consisted of 6,436 new-entrant households and 3,375 households that had participated in SNAP for about six months (for convenience, we refer to them as *six-month* households).[2] The IDI respondent sample was drawn from participants in six of the 30 states and consisted only of households with children. IDI respondents were offered an incentive of a $30 gift card to a local store for completing the interview.

From the set of 30 States participating in the SNAPFS telephone survey, we selected those in which to conduct IDIs using an algorithm designed (1) to achieve a higher degree of geographic diversity than we would through a random selection of States, and (2) to produce enough household respondents from the telephone survey to obtain 90 IDIs. Sample size was a particular concern, because IDIs were conducted only with households with children.

The first step in selecting the set of States in which to conduct SNAPFS IDIs was to define central geographic areas within States in which to conduct interviews. We used Core-Based Statistical Areas (CBSAs) to define geographic areas. CBSAs are county based and, for large metropolitan areas, usually cover the core city and the surrounding subcities and/or suburbs. In some cases, because of the county-based definition, they include semirural areas as well.

We selected the SNAPFS IDI sample of States prior to the SNAPFS telephone survey data collection period. Therefore, to ensure that an adequate sample of households would complete the baseline telephone interview, we estimated the number of households with children that would complete the telephone survey in each CBSA. This was equal to the product of (1) the percentage of the State's overall population residing in the CBSA, (2) a 50 percent factor to approximate the percentage of SNAP households that have children, and (3) the predicted number of completed household telephone interviews in the State. Because CBSAs can extend across State lines, we first subtracted the CBSA's population in adjoining States for each CBSA and then computed the percentage of the State's overall population residing in each CBSA.

We used a multistage design to select the sample of IDI households. In the first stage, we randomly selected two of the four Census regions of the country (northeast and south) to contribute "large" CBSAs and the other two regions (midwest and west) to contribute "small" ones. In the northeast and south, we randomly selected a CBSA from a set of the largest CBSAs in each region. In the midwest and west, we randomly selected a CBSA from a set of the smallest CBSAs in each region. The four CBSAs selected, and the States in which they are primarily located, were:

- Boston-Cambridge-Quincy, Massachusetts

- Houston-Sugarland-Baytown, Texas

---

[1] A comprehensive description of the SNAPFS telephone survey design is in that study's main report.

[2] The new-entrant households from October 2011 to February 2012 were asked to complete a follow-up interview about six months later, from April 2012 to early September 2012.

- Indianapolis-Carmel, Indiana

- Riverside-San Bernardino-Ontario, California

Within several weeks of completing interviews for the SNAPFS telephone survey in each of these four States, we began calling household respondents to request participation in the IDI survey and to schedule the interviews. The interviews, conducted between February 2012 and June 2012, usually took place in the respondents' homes. On occasion, at the request of the respondent, they were scheduled in a public place such as a restaurant, library, or community center. After several weeks of interviewing, the percentage of household respondents that had failed to show for the interview was larger than expected. Therefore, we decided to expand the initial geographic sample areas to include neighboring areas so that we could obtain a sufficient number of completed interviews. Additional interviews were conducted in Los Angeles, California; Dallas, Texas; Chicago, Illinois; and Providence, Rhode Island. In total, 251 households were contacted to participate in the survey. Of the 126 that agreed to participate we completed 90 interviews for an overall response rate of about 35.9 percent.[3] Respondents who during the initial telephone contact had agreed to participate but subsequently did not either were not home for the interview or, if the interview was to be held in a public place, did not show up for the interview and did not reschedule. About 62 percent of the IDI sample (56 of the 90 households) consisted of households that were new entrants at the time of the SNAPFS baseline survey. The distribution of completed interviews and no-shows by State is shown in Table I.1.

Table I.1. SNAPFS In- Depth Interview Survey Household Response Information

	Contacted	Scheduled Interviews	Completed Interviews
California	37	24	18
Illinois	45	19	15
Indiana	34	12	7
Massachusetts	34	14	12
Rhode Island	37	17	11
Texas	64	40	27
Total	**251**	**126**	**90**

B. Research Questions and Survey Topics

The objective of the SNAPFS IDI survey was to provide important insights into the challenges low-income families face and the coping strategies they deploy to remain food secure, and to inform the direction of future research on food security, including hypothesis generation and instrument design. The survey explored four main research questions:

---

[3] This response rate in this survey should be interpreted with caution. Our purpose was to draw a heterogeneous group of SNAP households with children, not to generate a representative sample. Indeed, our sample size is too small to claim representativeness, regardless of how respondents were recruited. To this end, we chose households at random from CBSAs and offered them the chance to participate. They had to do so in a very narrow window of time—usually a matter of two to five days—in which our interviewers were visiting their area of the state. Sample members that were not available during those times were often not able to be included as participants.

1. What are families' financial circumstances, hardships, and coping strategies generally?

2. What strategies do households use to meet family food needs?

3. What is the role of SNAP in helping households meet family food needs?

4. What challenges do families face that limit their ability to maintain food security?

To answer these questions, we developed an interview protocol based on prior, related qualitative studies of the financial lives of low-income households (Edin and Lein 1997; Mendenhall et al. 2012; Seefeldt 2008). The full interview protocol is in Appendix A. The questions were grouped into these categories:

- **Bills/expenditures.** Housing, utilities, communications, credit card, child care, transportation, medical insurance, food; strategies for meeting expenditures

- **Food security.** Bouts of food insecurity; coping strategies

- **Food dynamics and food eating.** With whom does respondent share food? Who cooks?

- **SNAP and food shopping.** Where does respondent typically shop? What does respondent buy?

- **Eating out and take-out.** When and under what circumstances do household members eat out or purchase take-out food?

- **SNAP and food security.** When did households first apply for SNAP? Other food programs they participate in; experiences in the SNAP office; discussions within the household about what to eat; household dynamics and associated challenges

- **Health, food, and nutritional knowledge.** Food allergies; health; healthy eating; children's diets

- **Expenditures and income.** Seasonal changes in expenditures; covering expenditures; household income; coping strategies when income low or expenditures high

C. Analysis

Narrative analysis is a powerful tool for describing important contextual details and for suggesting causal processes that could be shaping behavior. While the IDIs resemble semistructured conversations, we applied systematic, consistent analysis to translate the interviews into research findings.

The IDIs produced roughly 50 pages of transcribed interview data for each respondent; for a total of about 4,500 pages of text. These transcribed data were coded systematically by theme; each theme relating to one of the central questions outlined above (for example, food coping strategies). Each thematic code was then systematically analyzed for content (i.e. identifying the frequency and range of food coping strategies employed). This analysis was largely descriptive. However, for each theme, we assessed whether there were especially large differences by food security level (food secure, low food security, very low food security) and by race/ethnicity (non-Hispanic white, non-Hispanic black, Hispanic, and Other). We note especially large differences in these variables in this report. For instance, in Chapter III we point to several especially notable differences in the kinds of events that trigger a shortfall in the financial resources needed to secure food across food security groups, and several fairly large differences in food-related coping strategies.

It is important to recognize that, as qualitative analyses which involve similar techniques have noted (Boyd et al. 2010; Clampet-Lundquist et al. 2011; Edin and Lein 2007; England and Edin 2007), a small qualitative study like this effort cannot make definitive causal claims or estimate the precise magnitude of the patterns we note. Rather, this analysis should be used as one resource to use to generate hypotheses about the mechanisms and processes that might underlie variations in food security, and inform the design of future research tools.

After audio recording and transcribing all the interviews, we reviewed the questions covered in the conversations and identified "codes", or topics with which to categorize respondents' answers. An example of a code is "SNAP use and experience". We then identified "themes", which are more detailed categories within each code. Examples of themes within "SNAP use and experience" include "SNAP and food shopping" and "nutrition education." The codes and themes within each code were:

- **General economic situation.** Income; expenses; government assistance; financial struggles; and financial coping strategies

- **Food security.** Food expenses; food hardship; food hardship coping strategies

- **SNAP use and experience.** SNAP amount; SNAP and food shopping; SNAP tenure; no SNAP; nutrition education; other food programs

- **Food purchasing.** Grocery store experience; eating out and take-out

- **Eating and food dynamics.** Meals; household sharing of meals

- **Healthy and unhealthy food.** Health issues; cultural food practices

- **Support ideas.** Ideas for changing elements of SNAP

We coded transcribed interviews by theme using Atlas.ti, a computer-assisted qualitative data analytic software package. Next, we created a report, consisting of dialogue from the interviews, for each theme. These reports were sorted by food security level and by race/ethnicity to ensure we could identify especially large differences across these groups. We then wrote an internal memorandum summarizing the analysis of each theme and its subthemes. To ensure consistency across the memos, a standard format was followed for each memo, and each report was carefully reviewed. The analysis memos served as the foundation of this qualitative report.

In this report, we qualify findings based on the prevalence of household responses by using words such as "many", "most", "almost", and so on. The following is a general guide for these phrases:

- "Virtually all" means more than 95 percent of respondents

- "Almost all" means more than 90 percent of respondents

- "Most" means more than two-thirds of respondents

- "Many" means more than half of respondents, but less than two-thirds of respondents

- "About half" means about 50 percent of respondents

- A "substantial minority" or "quite a few" mean less than half, but more than a third of respondents

- "Some" means less than a third of respondents

- "Almost none" means less than 10 percent of respondents

- "Virtually none" means less than 5 percent of respondents

D. Characteristics of the SNAPFS IDI Survey Sample

In this section, we present characteristics and circumstances of the IDI survey sample. This information was gathered at the time of the SNAPFS telephone interview and thus may not reflect all the household circumstances at the time of the IDI.

About 62 percent of the IDI sample (56 of the 90 households) consisted of households that were new entrants at the time of the SNAPFS baseline survey. By the time of the IDI, they had been participating for about one to two months. The remaining households had participated in SNAP for about six months at the time of the baseline survey, or about seven to nine months at the time of the IDI.

The majority (85 percent) of both new-entrant and six-month households were headed by a female (Table I.2). Respondents were, on average, in their mid-thirties. Close to 38 percent of respondents were Hispanic. Black, non-Hispanic respondents made up the second-most-common racial/ethnic group (31.1 percent), followed by white, non-Hispanic respondents (24.4 percent) and non-Hispanic-other respondents (11.1 percent). About 24 percent of respondents had not completed high school. A similar percentage had received a high school diploma or GED but had not progressed beyond high school. Almost 45 percent of respondents had some college.

Table I.2. Demographic Characteristics and Household Composition of Survey Participant Households and Household Heads

Percentage of Household Heads that are Female	84.4
Average Age (in years) of Household Head	34.6
Race/Ethnicity of Household Head	
Non- Hispanic, white	24.4
Non- Hispanic, black	31.1
Non- Hispanic, other	11.1
Hispanic	37.8
Highest Grade Completed of Household Head	
Less than high school	23.6
High school graduate (diploma or GED)	23.6
Some college	44.9
College and beyond	7.9
Households with Children	
Single adult	52.2
Multiple adults	47.8
Household Size	
1 Person[a]	0.0
2 Person	25.6
3 Person	33.3
4 Person	16.7
5 Person	12.2
6+ Person	12.2
Percentage of Households with an Elderly Member	5.6

Percentage of Households with a Disabled Member	17.8

Source: SNAP Food Security 2012, IDI Sample.

Note: Table entries are percentages unless otherwise indicated. All statistics are unweighted. Characteristics and circumstances were measured at the time of the SNAPFS telephone interview, which preceded the in- depth interview by one to three months.

ª Because the survey was administered only to households with children, all households contained at least two members.

This study was designed to interview only households with children. More than half the sample (52.2 percent) consisted of single-adult households with children, and households generally contained two people (25.6 percent) or three people (33.3 percent). A small percentage of households contained an elderly member (5.6 percent); a larger percentage contained a disabled person (17.8 percent).

As presented in Table I.3, 58.4 percent of respondents were not employed. Those that were employed were three times more likely to be employed full-time (31.5 percent) than part-time (10.1 percent). Over 70 percent of the sample households had monthly gross incomes below the poverty level.[4] More than one-fifth of households had zero income. Finally, nearly a quarter of households received financial support from friends or family. Some households also received Social Security benefits (15.7 percent), child support (14.6 percent), TANF (7.8 percent), SSI (6.8 percent), and unemployment insurance benefits (6.7 percent).

Table I.3. Employment Status, Household Income, and Sources of Income of Survey Participant Households and Household Heads

Employment Status of Household Head	
Employed full- time	31.5
Employed part- time	10.1
Not employed	58.4
Monthly Income as a Percentage of Poverty	
No income	22.2
1 to 50 percent	17.8
51 to 100 percent	31.1
101 to 130 percent	12.2
More than 130 percent	16.7
Percentage of Households with Income Type	
TANF	7.8
Social Security	15.7
Supplemental Security Income (SSI)	6.8
Unemployment insurance or worker's compensation benefits	6.7
Child support payments	14.6
Financial support from friends or family	23.3

Source: SNAP Food Security 2012, IDI Sample.

---

[4] This is measured as a household's gross income relative to the SNAP income eligibility standards for Fiscal Year 2011 [http://www.fns.usda.gov/snap/government/FY11_Income_Standards.htm]. The standards represent 100 percent of the poverty level for each household size and closely resemble the Department of Health and Human Services poverty guidelines.

Note: Table entries are percentages unless otherwise indicated. All statistics are unweighted. Characteristics and circumstances were measured at the time of the SNAPFS telephone interview, which preceded the in- depth interview by one to three months.

More than half the sample households had participated in SNAP prior to their current spell (Table I.4). Almost 40 percent of households received a SNAP benefit which exceeded $301; 24.1 percent had benefits between $201 and $300, and another quarter (27.9 percent) received between $101-200 dollars per month. Less than nine percent of the IDI sample (8.9 percent) received less than $100 per month.

Many households participated in other federal nutrition assistance programs as well: 71.2 and 61.7 percent of households with children aged 5 to 18 participated in NSLP and SBP, respectively, and 34.6 percent of households with women aged 15 to 45 or children under 5 participated in WIC.

Table I.4. Participation in SNAP and Other Food and Nutrition Assistance Programs by Survey Participant Households

Prior SNAP Participation	55.1
Benefit Amount	
$0 to $100	8.9
$101 to $200	27.9
$201 to $300	24.1
$301 or more	39.2
Percentage of Households with Children Aged 5 to 18 that Participate in NSLP	71.2
Percentage of Households with Children Aged 5 to 18 that Participate in SBP	61.7
Percentage of Households with Women Aged 15 to 45 or Children Aged less than 5 that Participate in WIC	34.6

Source: SNAP Food Security 2012, IDI Sample.

Note: Table entries are percentages unless otherwise indicated. All statistics are unweighted. Characteristics and circumstances were measured at the time of the SNAPFS telephone interview, which preceded the in- depth interview by one to three months.

Table I.5 presents the food security status of adults and children in the sampled households. Adult food security was measured using the 10-item adult scale of the food security module of the Current Population Survey, and children's food security was measured using the additional 8-item child food security module (Nord and Bickel 2002). Based on the adult measure, over a third (37.8 percent) of surveyed households were food secure, and 62.2 percent of households were food insecure. Of the food insecure group, 24.4 percent experienced low food security and 37.8 percent had very low food security. Based on the children's food security measure, 42.2 percent of households had children who experienced some food insecurity, with 21.1 percent of those having children with very low food security.

Table I.5. Adult and Child Food Security Status of Survey Participant Households

Adult Food Security Status	
Food secure	37.8
Food insecure	62.2
Food insecure with low food security	24.4
Food insecure with very low food security	37.8
Child Food Security Status	

Food secure	57.8
Food insecure	42.2
Food insecure with low food security	21.1
Food insecure with very low food security	21.1

Source: SNAP Food Security 2012, IDI Sample.

Note: Table entries are percentages unless otherwise indicated. All statistics are unweighted.

II. GENERAL FINANCIAL CIRCUMSTANCES AND THE ROLE OF SNAP IN BENEFICIARIES' FINANCES

A. Overview

This chapter outlines the broad contours of SNAP beneficiaries' economic lives—their monthly incomes, major expenses, and overall balance sheets. We find that the typical household reports that they have more "month" than money—their expenses exceed their income. Since few can live off past or future income, this budget imbalance has a profound effect on their financial lives. Belt tightening, juggling the bills, doubling up, asking relatives and friends for assistance, "hustling" and relying on credit are all ways in which families get by.

What is SNAP's role in the family's financial picture? For most, SNAP is the basic building block of the monthly budget, ensuring that a household has some resources set aside for the one item they cannot go without—food. SNAP also frees up vital cash that would have had to be spent on food to help bridge budget gaps in other areas. SNAP eases the financial tradeoffs families must make as they strive to bring their budgets into balance, and may stave off material hardship. Nonetheless, the families in this study do frequently run short of the financial resources needed to purchase all of the food that they need. We show that this is in part because families do not typically earmark cash resources for food—they are often fully allocated to other purposes.

B. Budgets Out of Balance

To get a rough sense of each household's typical monthly budget, we asked them to describe their five largest monthly expenses, and then probed for expenses in all major domains—rent, utilities, food, and transportation, and so on — last month and in the months immediately prior to construct a monthly average. The probing questions were designed to determine the amount spent and whether the household was struggling to meet that expense. For example, we asked "How about utilities—heat, light, water and sewer? Tell me about the last time you struggled to pay your any of these bills"; "What about your credit payments? Tell me about the last time you struggled to meet these payments"; and similar questions (see Appendix A for a list of all questions). We then asked them to describe all sources of revenue coming into the household over the past six months. "Now let's talk about how you cover these expenses. Tell me about all the resources—big and small—that came into the household last month." Interviewers were instructed to probe for exact monthly amounts, and to probe for formal and informal income (for example, financial help from family and friends, "under the table" jobs, and so on). Interviewers were also reminded to solicit information about income from all sources for all household members (for example, not to forget contributions from teenage children that might have a job, fathers of children, and so on). Interviewers also asked how household income varied over the past year and the last time the household went without income (Appendix A).

In this way, we were able to construct a typical monthly budget. When we compared income to expenses, we found that in the typical month, many households' expenses exceeded their income. Most households could point to at least one month in the recent past where they lacked the resources to pay all of their expenses. Even households who were consistently in the black seldom had much cash left over once basic needs were met. *This fundamental economic reality—the frequency of budget shortfalls—profoundly shaped the role SNAP played in families' economic lives. When income falls short of expenses, tradeoffs are required; not all the bills can be paid, or be paid on time.*

Accordingly, many were behind on credit card or other debt payments, and many routinely could not pay their utility bills on time; some reported recent interruptions in service. Loss of cable, internet, or cell phone service was even more common. And though families usually made paying their rent or mortgage a priority, quite a few had also missed or made late payments in the recent past. Several households in the study had recently been evicted or had left their apartments for the homes of family members because they could no longer pay the rent; doubling up was common among those in our sample.

C. Tradeoffs and Strategies

What tradeoffs must households make, and what strategies do they deploy, when there is not enough money to get through the month? Interviewers were provided with a series of closely related questions to guide the respondent through this conversation. For example, "A lot of people say there is a lot of month left at the end of the money. How about for you? Over the last year, how have you coped during time where money was tight? Tell me all about the last time that happened? What about the time before that? How do you typically cope when the money gets tight? Tell me about the last time you ran short of what you needed to pay for food. How did you cope? How about the time before that? What do you typically do when the food budget gets tight?"

We learned that they tighten their belts, juggle, double up, draw on their networks, "hustle," and pay with credit.

Belt tightening efforts include keeping the lights off and the shades pulled to avoid using air conditioning in the summer heat, washing the clothes less often, and dozens of other money-saving schemes. As the quote below shows, it can even involve driving to church less often.

> "I don't even go to church every Sunday, like I used to. I try and go every other Sunday.
>
> (Interviewer: Just so that you can keep down the driving?)
>
> Yes, seriously. And it has helped. Little things have added up to make a big difference.
>
> (Interviewer: Yes, and what other little things can you think of?)
>
> How often I wash clothes…, I use my neighbor's lawnmower to do my grass you know which is something I always had a yard guy to come in and [do]."[5]

Juggling—sometimes referred to as "robbing Peter to pay Paul"—involves keeping some creditors at bay while others' demands are satisfied. Ensuring that this strategy does not result in further hardship—losing electric and gas service or being evicted—requires considerable skill and takes up a surprising amount of respondents' energy and time. Stories of sympathetic landlords are unexpectedly common. Utility companies will also often "work with you," and hospitals often showed flexibility as well. Other creditors, however, were not so lenient. One respondent explained how she juggled her bills.

---

[5] P43: Low Food Security, Black Non-Hispanic, Female, Age 54, 2-person household

"I make it work somehow…. [The law says they can't turn your heat off in the winter months, but] you know that April 15th, [they start cutting your gas off]. So you know that up until then you have the time, you [can] make a payment plan with them. You try not to miss [your payments] and if you do miss [one] you call back again and get one more chance to do it…. I have had times when, because I have an illness…, I…call to avoid a shut off because I have a medical issue. So if something [comes up] I can do [that] every once in a while. I try not to use that [strategy] unless I'm really late…. And then my doctor will fax the paperwork over to them…. It buys me a little time."[6]

Another told us,

"Pretty much a lot of the places will work with us. Like our water bill we can pay it two months at a time because it is so little anyway. They will wait two months before they even give us shut off date. So we just pay that [bill] two months at a time. Regarding our rent, they are pretty lenient because people around us are on Section 8 [too], so they just understand that we are working on it and we just let them know and we just give them what we can on the due date and then they will let you settle up."[7]

We asked one respondent, "When you struggle financially, what do you do?" Her response summarized the philosophy of many who must juggle their bills: "Pay what we can and don't worry about the rest."[8]

Another was asked, "So tell me how you're able to cover all those expenses?" She told us: "How? You rob Peter to pay Paul. Something doesn't get paid this month. The light bill doesn't get paid this month but I'll pay the gas bill and then if you get on the payment plan you don't pay as much you end up paying $100 opposed to $200 or $300."[9]

Doubling up is a common tradeoff families make to bring their budgets into balance. There are a number of three-generation households (in one case, even four) in the sample where money is shared across generations and siblings, though most doubled-up subfamilies keep their finances separate. Usually members of the younger generations move in with a parent or grandparent, who is the most likely to have a stable place of residence or own a home. Such households are highly fluid—with siblings, uncles, aunts, and other relatives coming and going as economic fortunes fall and then rise. One respondent described her situation in this way: "[We] live with my mom and my sister, my nephew. It seemed like everyone moved back in with mom. . . . So that's our family for now."[10]

---

[6] P53: Food Secure, Black Non-Hispanic, Female, Age 49, 3-person household

[7] P36: Food Secure, White Non-Hispanic, Female, Age 19, 3-person household

[8] P38: Food Secure, Black Non-Hispanic, Female, Age 26, 3-person household

[9] P53: Food Secure, Black Non-Hispanic, Female, Age 49, 3-person household

[10] P27: Low Food Security, Hispanic, Female, Age 31, 5-person household

Note that this is almost never a household's preferred mode of living; most are eager to move out as soon as their finances will allow. Families often value their independence, but also seek to avoid the sharp tensions that can arise in these situations. We said to one respondent, "So a lot of families these days, they're doubling up; more than one family living together so they can kind of help each other out." She responded, "But that don't always work, because they either always fighting, or somebody going get killed, or got two women in the house always trying to run things, that stuff will never work."[11]

Even for those who are not doubled up and do not pool income, networks are a key method families use to ease monthly budget strain. Respondents are quick to note, however, that this strategy too has its limits and that not all have access to it, even if they have kin in close proximity. We asked one respondent, "So what do you do when you can't pay your bills?" She replied, "Well, right now . . . because of my sickness and stuff, my mother and my sisters are trying to help me out as much as they can. But there is only so much that they can do after they get tired of helping out."[12]

Another explained,

> "[My family lives here in] Chicago, yes…. But they are the type that [say], 'You were the one who chose to be a mother, so you deal with it. Don't try to push your responsibility to nobody else.' Because of that, and that way of thinking, which is negative, it shows no type of support emotionally or economically. It's why I struggle—because I feel alone."[13]

For those with access to credit, credit cards help to smooth consumption when the monthly budget is in the red; but this is a strategy that is fraught with pitfalls. One respondent described the following scenario:

> "I was paying [my monthly balance in full]—I was spending $200, $300, then I'd pay it off. Then I'd put a little more on there, [but] then I just [couldn't keep] up. I didn't have no way to pay it off. I couldn't get no extra jobs to do this and that for nobody. Nobody wanted me to do nothing. I said, 'Lord why you punishing me like this? What did I do? I'm just trying to survive.' Then I'd get school clothes on the card and [because the bills] was just coming hitting me left and right…. I just couldn't believe I went through five cards, five credit cards."[14]

"Hustling" is a means to ease budget strain that includes a variety of entrepreneurial activities such as pawning jewelry or other valuables, selling plasma, gathering aluminum cans and other materials that can be redeemed for cash, or doing side work such as styling or braiding hair. One respondent explained her strategy for coping with financial hardship as follows:

> "I had a wedding ring I had to pawn, and Ed got me that about five years ago, but it had to go to the pawnshop because we needed some necessities…. [There were also]

---

[11] P54: Very Low Food Security, Black Non-Hispanic, Female, Age 44, 3-person household

[12] P57: Low Food Security, Hispanic, Female, Age 42, 6-person household

[13] P58: Very Low Food Security, Hispanic, Female, Age 28, 3-person household

[14] P55: Very Low Food Security, Black Non-Hispanic, Female, Age 40, 8-person household

several things that he had had to [pawn], like [his] tools, and they had to go to the pawn shop, because [were] struggling with food."[15]

Again, these strategies have limits, as illustrated by the comment of the following respondent, who told us: "I don't have anything worth pawning anymore."[16]

D. The Role of SNAP

SNAP considerably eased the tradeoffs families had to make when their budgets were in the red. It enabled households to reallocate cash resources they would otherwise have spent on food to other pressing obligations such as the light bill, a student loan payment, or even the rent. Many families credit the SNAP program with alleviating or averting hardship in a wide variety of domains; suggesting that it not only aids in ensuring food security but may help households to avoid other forms of material hardship as well. Several respondents refer to it as a "lifesaver." It is the basic building block of most of their budgets—the stream of resources that can be counted on, to meet their most basic material need each month. However, even with SNAP, households still struggle financially, make difficult financial tradeoffs, and go without; most continue to invest emotional energy, time, and creativity as they struggle to survive.

Financial difficulties occur even though most families receive significant means-tested transfers in addition to SNAP. Many claim the Earned Income Tax Credit and have enrolled their children in the State Child Health Insurance Program (SCHIP), and some receive Medicaid or are enrolled in a state-sponsored medical insurance program to cover their own health needs. TANF and housing subsidies are not as common, but some receive these as well. This is not to say that these safety net programs are unimportant. In fact, many respondents spontaneously testified to the significance of such programs in staving off hardship and promoting their family's well-being. This is especially true in regard to SNAP.

One respondent offered the following narrative about the role of SNAP in ensuring her family's financial wellbeing:

> "It is very difficult, very difficult. I am working…part time. I'm a single mom of two, and it seems like nothing is ever enough. No matter how many hours I put in it's not enough for what I need at home. I thank God that at least [I have] the SNAP benefits. It's the only way I can make it. Other than that, I wouldn't have anything to eat."[17]

We discuss respondents' views of the SNAP program more fully in Chapter V.

Households receiving SNAP are, by definition, living close to the economic margin. Parents often believe food purchases ought to take top priority. To keep their children from going without, they may forgo paying some bills to purchase food. But despite their willingness to tighten their belts and make tradeoffs, most are unable to protect enough of their cash resources from the press

---

[15] P37: Very Low Food Security, Other, Female, Age 66, 3-person household

[16] P77: Very Low Food Security, White Non-Hispanic, Female, Age 25, 2-person household

[17] P58: Very Low Food Security, Hispanic, Female, Age 28, 3-person household

of other financial demands. They do not typically set aside, or "earmark" a portion of their cash income for food, even though SNAP benefits rarely stretch to cover the whole month. SNAP seems to take concerns about securing enough food "off the table" when households decide how to allocate their scarce cash; nearly all of their cash resources ends up being earmarked for other purposes. Thus, financial shortfalls related to food are often a recurring problem, as we'll show in the next chapter.

E. Chapter II Summary

Budget shortfalls spark a cycle of juggling financial obligations. The pressure of the cycle is alleviated, but not in full, by a household's entry into the SNAP program. Families use SNAP benefits to help ease the impact when expenses exceed income. SNAP benefits enable families to maintain food as a spending priority—virtually all of the SNAP resources are spent on food—while not falling as far behind in meeting their other obligations—rent, utilities, transportation, and educational or medical debt—as they otherwise might. Only one respondent in the study reported that she occasionally exchanged her SNAP benefits for cash.

Financial struggle occurs despite access to the social safety net, as well as the significant, and sometimes valiant, efforts families make at belt tightening: keeping the lights off to lower the utility bill, clipping coupons and traveling to multiple stores to get the best bargains, and even forgoing a trip to church to save on fuel.

In addition, families often "juggle": they pay some of their bills while negotiating with or even defaulting on other creditors. These practices, besides incurring late fees and reconnection charges, put many households in serious debt—debt that constrains future access to credit. Other strategies include doubling up with relatives, gleaning other kinds of network support, running up credit cards, and bringing in small amounts of extra cash via entrepreneurial activities such as braiding hair or selling plasma. However these ways of dealing with overburdened monthly budgets have sharp limitations and are not equally available to all.

To summarize: in most cases, families' best efforts to make ends meet—aided but not alleviated by SNAP benefits—still fall short.

III. FINANCIAL SHORTFALLS RELATED TO FOOD AND COPING STRATEGIES AMONG THE FOOD SECURE AND FOOD INSECURE

A. Overview

Families experiencing financial shortfalls related to food over the prior six months identified four sources of the difficulties they faced. In order of frequency, these include: (1) temporal variation, defined as changes across years, seasons, or months, in income or expenses; (2) unusually high recurring expenses; (3) abrupt changes in income and expenditure; (4) and the unexpected loss of or reduction in government benefits.

As one would expect, there is a strong association between not having enough SNAP or cash on hand to buy all of the food the family needs and the level of food security a household was experiencing at the time of the survey. We analyze similarities and differences in both the events that produce these shortfalls and the coping strategies employed over the preceding six months by families' food security level ("food secure", "low food security" and "very low food security"). Several large differences between these groups emerge from this analysis.

Because the experience of these budget shortfalls related to food was so common, coping strategies of one kind or another were employed by nearly all households in our sample, sometimes in the face of a shortfall and other times to avoid it. We include both the reactive and proactive coping strategies households relied upon when faced with these shortfalls.

Many triggers for financial hardship were common across demographic and economic groups. For example, there was no clear pattern in temporal variations—the most common trigger of financial shortfalls—by food security level. Some were specific to those in the "very low food security" group. Those in this group are by far the most likely to experience financial shortfalls related to food because of a disruption in government benefits. Most typically, this relates to the loss of or reduction in SNAP benefits. Notably, no household in the food secure group reported that an unexpected drop in government benefits triggered a spell of financial hardship.

Changes in SNAP benefits can occur because income or household composition changes, because families fail to comply in full, or on time, with program requirements, or because of administrative error. Respondent households often cite administrative error, but this may or may not actually be the case. Those in the "very low food security" group are also roughly twice as likely to experience a financial shock—an abrupt rise in expenses or fall in resources. High recurring expenses were also more common among the less food secure.

Families described a variety of coping strategies they used to respond to, or avoid financial shortfall. These coping strategies include: (1) reducing food intake; (2) reducing food quality or variety (stretching); (3) accessing family networks for food and cash support; (4) and pro-active preventative strategies like aggressive sales shopping, couponing, or meal planning.

Reducing food intake, skipping meals, and changing the type of food the household consumes (trading meat for ramen noodles at the end of the month, for example) were much more common strategies among the less food secure, though these coping mechanisms were used by at least a substantial minority of all food security groups.

In addition, many of the food secure households benefit from frequent invitations to relatives' homes for meals and receive contributions of groceries and cash from their family and friends.

These households can usually rely on their networks to provide cash, groceries, or meals routinely when SNAP benefits run out toward the end of the month. The less food secure have less access to these network resources. In fact, those in the very low food security group often explicitly state that they do not have networks that are able or willing to provide. And even those in the very low food security group who do have networks who are willing to provide often say they cannot rely on them, usually because the potential donor is in a financial situation similar to their own.

Conversely, networks are sometimes a drag on the resources of those in the "very low food insecure" group, but not among the food secure. Those who felt they must share their SNAP with others not in the official SNAP household were virtually all in the very low food security group, suggesting that when respondents' network members are even more needy than the respondents themselves, it can be costly to a household's own wellbeing.

Finally, those households who are the least food secure are also the least likely to engage in key forms of proactive coping: carefully researching the best prices on particular products, traveling to multiple grocery stores—sometimes a considerable distance away—several times a month to capitalize fully on sales, and carefully planning the meals around what is on sale rather than on the households' food preferences. Managing one's food budget in this way requires considerable skill, and this skill is often richly evident in the narratives of the food secure but less so among the food insecure. It also requires some measure of stability in one's economic and living situations, a level of stability that was less common among the very low food insecure.

Use of food pantries, a strategy adopted by a large minority of respondents, did not vary significantly by food security level.

B. Sources of Financial Shortfalls Related to Food

Here we focus specifically on episodes where a household runs short of SNAP or cash resources for securing all of the food they need. We aggregate the broad range of the triggers of these financial shortfalls into four categories, arranged in order of frequency: (1) temporal variation in resources or expenses; (2) unusually high recurring expenses, (3) unexpected and sudden financial shocks in income or expenditure, and (4) loss or reduction in benefits from government programs.

Temporal Variation

For SNAP recipients, as for almost all Americans, there is a temporal dimension to fat and lean times. For low-wage workers, tax credits like the EITC that are redeemed in late winter or early spring usually provide a significant windfall of cash, while holidays can place extraordinary strain on the family budget. But there are temporal variations of other kinds: jobs with a seasonal dimension, summers when the kids are out of school, the extra expenses that accrue over holidays—particularly Christmas, and the ubiquitous shortfall in resources that occurs toward the end of the month. Interviewers asked, "Some times of the year are easier on the food budget than others. For example, some families tell us it's a lot easier in months when their kids are getting free breakfast and lunch at school. Others say it's easier during the summer, when kids are off visiting relatives." Then the interviewer asked, "How about for you?" Interviewers also asked: what are the toughest times to get by food-wise; what bills go up and down depending on the season; and how has your household income varied over the past year (e.g. is anyone only able to work some months during the year)? Interviewers were instructed to probe for specific amounts and to ask about increased expenses during the winter months due to holiday shopping and heating bills (if cold climate) as well as increases in food expenses during the summer due to kids being out of school. Appendix A contains the full set of questions asked.

Temporal variation in resources or expenses is the most frequently cited trigger of financial hardship, described by nearly six in ten (59 percent) respondents. In particular, respondents point to summers and to holidays like Christmas—when they are expected to purchase presents and/or special clothing for their children—along with their children's birthday months, as the toughest times of the year on the budget. In the summer months, when children are generally not in school, households must provide the breakfasts and lunches their children usually receive free at school. One mother of a teenage boy works very long hours at her job and describes the strain summer puts on her food budget as follows:

> "Summers are horrible, because [he] was home alone from 9 a.m. to 10 p.m. eating. And then I would come home and make like a tray of chicken thighs and mashed potatoes and I'd go lay down for like a second, and then I'd come out and all the chicken is gone and there's like a bowl of mashed potatoes left. I'm like 'What the hell!' He's like, 'You ate, right?' I'm like, 'No'. And so he's like, 'I'm sorry'. I'm like, 'Whatever'."[18]

Unusually High Recurring Expenses

Some households experience food hardship because of recurring expenses that are higher than those of most families. High recurring expenses triggered recent financial hardship for about a third (31 percent) of respondents in our study. These budget-breakers can include unusually high costs for fuel for those who have to commute a long way to work or school or those who must travel from place to place as a part of their job, such as landscapers and house cleaners. One respondent, who worked for a landscaping firm, told us about the tradeoff decisions she has to make, as well as the strategies she deploys to cope:

> "I always have to have enough for gas so like if I have $100 and I need gas in the truck to go to work the next day or I need to [fill up the tank] I'll even get to the point where it'll affect food purchases, which it has done in the last month.... I had to do without buying food in order to put gas in the truck to go to work the next day.... I get Food Stamps on the 5th.... Three weeks later, the food stamps are gone so at that point, the food's coming out of my pocket and if I have money, I have to make that choice you know? I have to have gas in order to work to make more money. I can do without meat, for example, which we've done many, many times. I eat a lot less meat now than I ever did in my whole life because it's so expensive. Maybe we'll eat macaroni and cheese and peas or something. There's no meat so that we have gas."[19]

Other high recurring expenses include expensive prescription drugs not covered by an insurance plan, or special foods required because of diabetes, food allergies, and other such conditions. One respondent told us,

---

[18] P40: Very Low Food Security, White Non-Hispanic, Female, Age 33, 3-person household

[19] P7: Very Low Food Security, White Non-Hispanic, Female, Age 41, 4-person household

"I was having to choose between medicine to stay out of pain and function and try to raise my ten year old because there are so many things I can't do with him now like I did my other two sons. I'm afraid that's all [he] is going to remember of me, that his mom was sick. So yeah, there have been times this year, the past year where there really wasn't enough to eat and I felt really badly about it."[20]

Another also discussed the impact of her health challenges on her food budget:

"I have health issues so some things I have [to eat]—yogurt I have to eat a lot of yogurt. If I get too much yogurt then I'll run short on something else. I'm underweight so they're trying to fatten me up with all of this stuff. And I'm like, 'I can't afford that!'"[21]

Some households report housing costs that are much higher than the average in the sample. Generally, these respondents are downwardly mobile homeowners or renters living in high-priced urban areas. One respondent said her rent was so high that "a lot of times like, we don't have enough for food. And, so that's kind of hard."[22]

Others respondents have unusually high grocery bills because they cook not only for their own families but also for others not covered by SNAP. Having "extra mouths to feed" was by far the most cited reason for food hardship within the "high recurring expense" category. More than one in five (22 percent) of all respondents mentioned this as a trigger of a spell of food hardship.

Sometimes children and grandchildren move in, or call saying there is nothing to eat in the house. Among African American households at least, strong norms often appeared to dictate that whoever has food resources must provide meals for all. One such respondent explained, "When I cook everybody eats. It's not like only my children can eat. My grandson is here so I'm never going to exclude him. His dad, my son is here. I'll never exclude him, you know what I mean...?"[23] Another related the following: "We had [my son] Juan move in so there is one more mouth to feed. There are now two extra mouths to feed. There are other expenses also like water, electric. His son will eat us out of house and home."[24]

Even those not doubled up sometimes feel compelled to give their scarce food resources to a family member in need, particularly if there are children in the household. One respondent explained his situation in this way: "My son sometimes calls because he has kids, and he said, 'Mom do you have a piece of meat or something I could borrow?' I get it because you know, I can't say no. And I say, 'Yeah, yeah.' Because he's got kids, it ain't just...him."[25]

---

[20] P78: Very Low Food Security, White Non-Hispanic, Female, Age 54, 2-person household

[21] P70: Very Low Food Security, White Non-Hispanic, Female, Age 54, 2-person household

[22] P37: Very Low Food Security, Other, Female, Age 66, 3-person household

[23] P18: Very Low Food Security, Hispanic, Female, Age 38, 4-person household

[24] P68: Very Low Food Security, Hispanic, Female, Age 31, 6-person household

[25] P37: Very Low Food Security, Other, Female, Age 66, 3-person household

A few feel compelled to share what they have with neighbors who are worse off even than they are—people who are ill or homeless, or who have no food. Sharing what one has fits with these respondents' moral and religious beliefs. One explained, "And sometimes…I'll feed this [homeless] guy right here named Mike…, I'll give him some food. Or I'll give [to] the lady straight ahead. And she's got cancer…and so I give her food too. You know, but the way I see it, God gives. And when he does, you'll be multiplied more."[26] Another said, "Last month, I, you know, used my food stamps to help my friends, you know, they didn't have no food so it's like okay I got $600 of food stamps, well, I can struggle a little bit to help somebody else."[27] And a third echoed the willingness to "struggle a little" in order to help someone else in need, "If somebody that's hungry and needs something to eat or whatever, if that's my last can of soup, I would still give it to them."[28]

Notably, all the cases above were in the very low food security group, which suggests that, compared to the networks of the households with greater food security, the networks of the least food secure households contain more relatives and neighbors who are even worse off. The least food secure are about twice as likely as the other groups to report an episode of food hardship triggered by high recurring costs, for example (44 percent versus 20 and 23 percent of those with low food security and the food secure, respectively).

Abrupt Changes in Income and Expenditure

There are two kinds of abrupt changes in income or expenditure that induce financial hardship. The first is a sudden loss of <u>income</u> from a reduction of hours at work, job loss, temporary work interruptions due to childbirth or illness, the loss of a wage-earning partner, or the reduction or loss of cash or in-kind support from an ex-partner, family member, or friend. The second involves an unexpected <u>expense</u>, such as a car breaking down, a jump in one's health insurance premium, or unexpected overdraft fees from the bank. More than one in four (27 percent) respondents pointed to a financial shock of one kind or another as being a trigger of recent financial hardship. Sometimes, these financial "shocks" come one right after the other, leading to a financial cascade. While 14 percent of the food secure reported a recent financial shock, 28 percent of the low food secure and fully a third of the very low food secure did so.

A Sudden Loss of Income

Some respondents experienced unexpected job losses, which altered their financial situations dramatically. We asked one householder to describe any unexpected events that had triggered recent hardship. She replied,

> "Losing my job. I didn't have Food Stamps so it…really hurt. I had spent the last $400. I had got one check—the very last check I had got was for like $600. I already knew I had to move and I already talked to the apartment complex. 'This is happening. I'm going to try and be out of here by the end of the month because there is no way I'm going to be able to pay you guys this much rent.' I had…the

---

[26] P37: Very Low Food Security, Other, Female, Age 66, 3-person household

[27] P42: Very Low Food Security, Black Non-Hispanic, Female, Age 46, 4-person household

[28] P54: Very Low Food Security, Black Non-Hispanic, Female, Age 44, 3-person household

utility bill that I needed to pay, so I paid that utility bill and then I went ahead and I bought food with the last money that I had."[29]

Interruptions in employment due to pregnancy and childbirth were a common cause of hardship as well. One respondent told us:

"I'm a person who's very responsible at work. I mean, I worked before I had her. But you see, I had to quit the job because I got pregnant…and I had vomiting and [was] nauseous, so I couldn't work. I was going to end up throwing up at the store or something. And I couldn't let that happen…. When I was working, we were doing all right. We weren't doing so bad because I was getting paid $7.25 [an hour]. Everything was working out fine. But now that I don't work, we're stuck. We don't know what we can do."[30]

One young mother said it was the hardship that resulted from lost wages that motivated her to apply for SNAP, and claimed that SNAP alleviated some of the hardship she believed her family would have otherwise faced during her pregnancy. "I had [my daughter] November 20 . . . but I had to take off two weeks earlier just because I couldn't even [stand up]. So I had to apply for Food Stamps and by the grace of God they gave them to me. They help so much because if it weren't for that, we wouldn't be able to eat."[31]

Other hardships were due to interruptions to work because of a health problem (either the respondent or a family member). Two respondents reported broken ankles that prohibited work for a time; cancer treatments prevented another from working; and one mother could not return to work three months after her daughter was born, as she had planned, because her newborn required surgery and long-term hospitalization. This respondent described her situation as follows:

"I just had my daughter and I [had been] working full time [up until she was born]. They fired me because [I couldn't go back to work after three months due to the fact that] my daughter had surgery…. I had applied for an extension on my FMLA and I asked for another month and they couldn't—they said, 'No.' So they fired me. And I had…a hard pregnancy. I was in and out the hospital all the time [but I still stayed employed]. And I was unemployed from November until—I still am."[32]

The loss of a wage-earning partner from divorce, death, breakup, or incarceration was a common hardship trigger.[33] One recent divorcee offers a typical narrative:

---

[29] P18: Very Low Food Security, Hispanic, Female, Age 38, 4-person household

[30] P35: Food Secure, Hispanic, Female, Age 20, 3-person household

[31] P38: Food Secure, Black Non-Hispanic, Female, Age 26, 3-person household

[32] P38: Food Secure, Black Non-Hispanic, Female, Age 26, 3-person household

[33] An onset of doubling up could theoretically lead to hardship by increasing expenses, if the SNAP beneficiary was the party providing shelter to destitute kin. However, in our data, our families were typically on the receiving, and not the giving, end of such exchanges. A new baby in the household might also cause financial distress. However, families almost never point to expenses related to childbirth as a source of financial hardship. This is perhaps because the costs are minimal at first and largely subsumed by Medicaid, the WIC program, and network aid.

"It was more difficult [after the divorce] because at that time my mortgage was sky high and I had to try to juggle that which I had to do some other things. I traded my—I had a Suburban I traded that in. I downsized a lot. I downsized. I just regrouped. Food, we didn't—they weren't hungry, no. Bills won't get paid [before the kids go hungry]."[34]

In six cases, the incarceration of a wage-earning partner was the primary cause of a recent or ongoing hardship. A mother of one relates the following story:

"My baby's dad, he is in jail facing a charge that was crazy and was false. False accusations. So I got pregnant at 17, had my little girl at 18. I'm 19 now and it's just been hard. Being a single parent has just been hard so I've been trying to do everything on my own and do what I can for her and survive…while he's not here."[35]

In another case, a partner's income was lost when a mother learned her partner was working for a drug cartel. Fearing for her children's safety, she evicted him from the house.

Interruptions to child support payments, another typical hardship trigger, can occur because of nonpayment or a child aging out of eligibility. One respondent describes her situation as follows:

"He's supposed to pay child support but he doesn't want to so he keeps moving and changing jobs. So it takes 30 days for me to not get a check before I can report it. Then it takes 60 days before they can do something about it. And then they do a social security search, which usually takes another 30-60 days. So now we're on four months and I'm calling every day. They're getting upset with me and I understand. But at the same time, he does this every other month. And then he'll get a job, they'll find him, and he'll work there for like three months and then leave. And it will take about four months to find him again."[36]

Hikes in Expenditures

A car breaking down can constitute a significant financial shock to a low-income household. Given the unreliability of the cars most respondents drive, the incidence is not low. One respondent in this situation told us, "There was a time my car had broke down. I had to pay to get that fixed. It was around the 20th of the month, so no more food stamps, [and there was no money for food]."[37]

The following quote describes how an unexpected expense for a prescription drug can rob the food budget, leading to severe strain at the end of the month:

"[The] last week of the month is horrible because . . .if that week, anything happens, [you are going to have to go without]. For example, my son got mono four months

---

[34] P53: Food Secure, Black Non-Hispanic, Female, Age 49, 3-person household

[35] P59: Low Food Security, Black Non-Hispanic, Female, Age 22, 3-person household

[36] P40: Very Low Food Security, White Non-Hispanic, Female, Age 33, 3-person household

[37] P18: Very Low Food Security, Hispanic, Female, Age 38, 4-person household

ago [during that last week of the month], and he had to be seen and he had to have medication and so you think, 'Okay, I've got $200 for food.' [If] you go spend $88 on that and now what are you going to do? Food or medication? Well I'm going to go ahead and spend my food money [for the medication] because he has to have the medication and I'll just work more or I'll take it from somewhere else."[38]

A hike in an insurance premium triggered food hardship for another, who explained, "Where I work at, they sell the place [to new owners], so I think - I don't know, I think it was - I started to struggle right then because before I didn't have to pay my insurance, my health insurance. They used to pay it for me, so since then I've been struggling more."[39]

From these examples, it is clear that financial shocks can be one-time events—the car breaks down—or become recurring obligations and have more permanent effects—a sudden increase in insurance premiums that will become an ongoing monthly challenge.

Financial Cascades

In several cases, one or more hardship-inducing events cascade, creating cumulative financial challenges. One respondent offers the following example:

"Well, four years ago my husband died of cancer also, so four years ago that happened to me, and that brought me down. Yeah, and then again three years ago, a year after [I lost my husband], I lost my job…because the company closed down. So I lost it and I was on unemployment for like two years and then unemployment stopped. And then I tried to get a job but it's really hard to get a job right now…. And then I got stuck with the cancer treatments and all that, so it's been hard to go back [to work]."[40]

Another respondent told us,

"[What has been difficult] is my job [loss], and then also the dad leaving us…. Yeah, he left us when [my daughter] was like eight months or whatever…. [And then there was when I was incarcerated for fighting that dude who was stalking me, and I lost custody of my children]. Yeah. It's always some dude! I'm telling you…! They are all trouble except for the one I am with now."[41]

Loss or Reduction in SNAP and Other Government Benefits

In addition to SNAP, recipients often rely on other government programs like Unemployment Insurance, WIC, and occasionally TANF. When there is an interruption or reduction in any of these benefits, it can cause a spell of food hardship. The loss or reduction in SNAP was the most frequently mentioned disruption that triggered food hardship. As we will discuss further in Chapter

---

[38] P7: Very Low Food Security, White Non-Hispanic, Female, Age 41, 4-person household

[39] P15: Low Food Security, Hispanic, Female, Age 29, 6-person household

[40] P57: Low Food Security, Hispanic, Female, Age 42, 6-person household

[41] P14: Food Secure, White Non-Hispanic, Female, Age 30, 3-person household

V, these often-unexpected changes in SNAP benefits were among respondents' primary frustrations with the SNAP program. The loss or reduction in government benefits was the *least frequently* cited cause of financial hardship across the sample (identified by 17 percent of respondents), yet it is the source of financial shortfalls that is most clearly associated with very low levels of food security, as we discuss further below.

As indicated earlier, social programs, especially SNAP, often play a vital economic role in our respondents' lives. When benefits are lost, or even merely reduced, respondents report that household finances are altered dramatically. We discuss in Chapter VI some of the profound impacts of such losses. One respondent describes how a reduction in SNAP forced her to reallocate to food the cash she had set aside for rent and other bills:

> "The problem, as I explained to you, last month—they gave me all of SNAP completely the month of April and this month they gave me only a portion. For example, what is the date? Is it the 15th? The 15th and everything is gone. It's all gone from here to the end [of the month]. I am now taking it out of my pocket from the little bit that is left from my pay. And on top of that I need to keep aside a weekly amount for the rent and for the rest of the expenses that I explained to you— the gas, the electricity, the cable, and [I'm not able to] because the Food Stamps are all gone now."[42]

Families also offer similar narratives to describe the impact on the budget when children age out of TANF or survivors' benefits. Few say they anticipated the benefit reductions; the rules of the program and the methods used to calculate both eligibility and benefit levels are often not well understood. Thus, clients tend to view transfer programs as capricious, granting and withholding assistance based on whims and technicalities rather than on a family's level of need. As we will show in Chapter V, even in cases where beneficiaries do at least partly understand the rules and methods, they can be perceived as unfair.

One respondent reported that she got a temporary job, failed to report it to SNAP within the required 10-day period, and was sanctioned off SNAP for a full year, even though the job had lasted only three weeks. When we met her, she had been without SNAP for several months and was down to just a few items of food in her cupboards. Another said that the SNAP office closed her case, insisting that she procure a letter from a prior employer documenting the fact that she had been laid off from her prior job. The employer proved hard to track down. During that time, she says,

> "...it became difficult for us to purchase food. We would run out of food, and I had to wait until he got paid on Friday and we would go to the supermarket and could only spend $80 for the week, and that didn't last long. I had to have breakfast, lunch and dinner available for my daughter when she was off from school [for the summer] and [for] me, because we were home the whole day. My husband only ate dinner when he got home. So when I saw that it became more difficult for us to have food on the table, I was motivated to really seek out my former employer to write the letter for me to state that I no longer was employed with the company. I pretty

---

[42] P74: Low Food Security, Hispanic, Male, Age 57, 5-person household

much had to beg the social worker to reopen my case and the supervisor assigned a social worker for me and that's when my case was reopened."[43]

We heard many stories of how a recertification deadline that was missed by a day or even a couple of hours resulted in lost benefits for a full month. Sometimes, this was allegedly an error on a caseworker's part: lost paperwork and caseworker mistakes were frequent complaints. We also heard many stories about how time consuming recertification often was, and how difficult it was for workers to take time off from their jobs to wait in line for hours at the public aid office. One respondent who experienced this dilemma described her situation as follows:

"I was so stressed, going through a whole lot. I didn't have time to actually go into Public Aid and do the reinstatement for the SNAP benefits, so they cancelled it for me for two months straight. I really, really struggled. I struggled so much, I didn't know what else to do. Like, emergency food was worth enough for those two months, but I broke down through the phone. I didn't know what else to do. She told me, 'It's going to be maybe another two weeks before you get anything else,' and I cried."[44]

One respondent describes what happened when she missed a recertification deadline right before Christmas:

"December, Christmas season was pretty dry. It was pretty sad. We were not working as much—I was able to pay my rent and that was it. Um, the food stamp thing [wouldn't] start [again] until January…. December, yeah, we were…very, very tight. Even going out of the house [was pretty hard because] there was a lot of people out shopping [for Christmas presents] and for a 15 year old to see that he's just not going to get anything was horrible, it was heartbreaking. My six year old doesn't really comprehend what holidays are and getting presents and quality and brands or none of that. So, I mean, any small thing was okay. But when you just can't provide [nothing for a 15 year old], it's just, it was horrible. [Finding enough money for] food was a little bit tough that month."[45]

Fifteen households experienced a financial shortfall related to food due to this cause, but no food secure household did so, as compared to 16 percent of those with low food security and more than a fourth (28 percent) of those with very low food security. As noted earlier, nearly all these benefit reductions, interruptions, or losses occurred within the SNAP program. One respondent with very low food security described a time when her SNAP benefits were cut off because of an error that the SNAP office made, saying "My daughter and her boyfriend and their daughter all moved in and I got discontinued because the paperwork got put in the wrong place. The supervisor had to figure out everything."[46] It took some time for her benefits to be reinstated, and in the meantime she struggled to provide food for her family.

---

[43] P31: Very Low Food Security, Hispanic, Female, Age 30, 2-person household

[44] P58: Very Low Food Security, Hispanic, Female, Age 28, 3-person household

[45] P8: Very Low Food Security, Hispanic, Female, Age 32, 3-person household

[46] P64: Very Low Food Security, White Non-Hispanic, Female, Age 43, 6-person household

C. Coping Strategies

SNAP beneficiaries must employ coping strategies that are both reactive—to deal with food hardship—and proactive—to avoid it. Common reactive strategies included: restricting food intake, altering the kinds of foods consumed, turning to networks, and visiting food pantries. But many respondents also described a highly effective patterns of proactive coping: scouring the ads for sales, traveling from store to store several times a month to ensure the best bargains, and planning meals almost entirely around the sales.

Restricting Food Intake

Skipping meals is common among our respondents, so much so that some have gotten used to it and do not even consider it a hardship. Overall, 45 percent of cases reported limiting food intake as a strategy to stretch their food budget. However, almost two-thirds of very low food secure households (67 percent) resorted to this, versus 32 percent for the food secure and 24 percent for the low food secure. The following quote illustrates this point:

"(Interviewer: Tell me about the last time you or someone in your house had to skip a meal because there wasn't enough.)

I skip two meals a day.

(Interviewer: You're kidding! You only eat once a day? Is that by choice because of...?)

It's not by choice, it's more - I guess it was a choice at first, that it has become a habit now and I'm used to it. So I don't eat breakfast, and if I eat lunch I won't eat dinner because I'm still full.

(Interviewer: So you just got used to that.)

I got used to it.

(Interviewer: But it started because you didn't have enough?)

Exactly, because I didn't have [enough money for food]

(Interviewer: When was that?)

When I was struggling last year for those two months. It became a habit and I got used to it. Somehow I managed to program my own brain to not feel any hunger, I guess - my body to not feel any type of hunger."[47]

Another described a similar "habit" of skipping meals regularly:

---

[47] P58: Very Low Food Security, Hispanic, Female, Age 28, 3-person household

"Me, personally, sometimes I'll skip meals especially on days when I go to work; then you don't feel it because you're working. I've skipped meals. We really don't eat at family's house very much. My mom, she's still kind of struggling, and his mom lives too far. I guess we're just winging it, really. I guess a couple of months ago we did [run out of food]. We actually had one pack of noodles left and then we ran out. We really didn't know what to do and I think that's when his mom might have pitched in and she got us something. It was stressful. We really didn't know what to do."[48]

Many respondents' stories emphasize that the sacrifices they are making by skipping meals are to ensure that their children get adequate food. One respondent explains how she limits her food intake to make sure her son has food to eat:

"I worry more about my family making sure that they have enough food. And then I'll get like, because we have chips, I work in the emergency room, I get like the crackers. I've been living off crackers or Ramen noodles. The good thing about it is, my doctor is very upset with me, he says my body is in starvation mode, so it's holding onto everything that I eat, because it doesn't know when I'm going to eat again. And I tell him there's nothing I can do about that. For now this is how it is. But I've actually gotten really used to eating like once a day, and then if I drink a lot right before I eat, then I don't eat that much and then I give my son my leftovers."[49]

Another tells a similar story of prioritizing her son, and skipping meals to do so,

"Oh yeah, [SNAP] doesn't cover a month. There is no way. It doesn't cover a month, not with a growing ten year old. There is no way. Half the time I don't eat. I'll live on coffee and pain medication. That sounds awful but I can go without food. I need to lose some weight anyway. That's not the way to do it, I know, but when it comes to [him] eating or me, it's going to be [him] every time."[50]

Changing the Type of Food Consumed

Nearly half (46 percent) of the respondents in this sample say they regularly change the type of food they eat toward the end of the month in order to get by—generally resorting to Top Ramen, potatoes, pasta, and other cheap starches that "stretch," as well as canned goods. This strategy is especially common in the very low food security group, although it is a strategy employed by respondents in all the food security groups. Top Ramen comes up again and again in these narratives as the fall-back when food gets tight. Many report that to get by, they "just go out and buy noodles [Top Ramen]" which cost only pennies a pack, or draw on a reserve of ramen, canned goods, or other non-perishables they have stockpiled in past months as insurance against food shortages. One respondent relates how she ate cereal without the milk the last time her food budget ran dry:

---

[48] P41: Very Low Food Security, Black Non-Hispanic, Female, Age 23, 2-person household

[49] P40: Very Low Food Security, White Non-Hispanic, Female, Age 33, 3-person household

[50] P78: Very Low Food Security, White Non-Hispanic, Female, Age 54, 2-person household

"During that time when I didn't have no food, I didn't go asking anybody. I had plenty of peanut butter and jelly in there; I had a lot of canned goods [and non-perishables]. I didn't have any meats at all, no frozen food or nothing.

(Interviewer: So you just changed what you ate?)

I changed what I eat. I'm making some tuna, something I didn't like; cereal, but without milk, so whatever I had and I just trying to you know just do what I had to do as far as eating. What, that was like the worst time ever, yes."[51]

Another told us she knew her stock had really run low when she noted that she had only one serving of Top Ramen left. To cope, her family ate hamburger helper "minus the meat."

"I looked in the kitchen and there is nothing in the refrigerator, there's like no milk or nothing. And I'm like there's ketchup, mustard, mayonnaise, and jelly. I'm like, 'What the hell happened?' And it's nowhere near Friday [when SNAP comes in], and the Ramen—we had one bag of Ramen left. No more hamburger, no more meat in the freezer at all. There's a frozen vegetable in the freezer and that was it. And so I was just like this is going to be interesting. So I had some of the, you know like the Hamburger Helper things, and I just made those minus the meat."[52]

Some families keep a reserve of cheap non-perishables as insurance against the predictable end-of-the-month shortfall. One such respondent colorfully explains that like a camel, a household must keep a reserve "so you won't die."

"March I ran out of stamps on the 23rd. So I had a whole week, but I go to my reserve in my pantry, all my stuff that I store. I like frozen vegetables but I will keep canned goods. That's when you make spaghetti. I keep stuff you can survive on, beans and rice, I actually make those from scratch. But in a can I like Bush beans, something like that. I keep a couple of cans of chili, for chili dogs or nachos, things like that. That's why a camel has a hump, for reserve. You just reserve [so] you won't die."[53]

Another respondent describes a similar strategy:

"You know [how you deal with the end of the month?] You stock up on things that won't spoil and you know you're better off because when you don't have food stamps, at least you have raviolis. You know or something that, you know, when you do run out of food, at least you have something for emergencies like [what you would need if] a hurricane comes and you're stuck in your house for 3 days."[54]

---

[51] P54: Very Low Food Security, Black Non-Hispanic, Female, Age 44, 3-person household

[52] P40: Very Low Food Security, White Non-Hispanic, Female, Age 33, 3-person household

[53] P51: Very Low Food Security, Hispanic, Female, Age 53, 4-person household

[54] P83: Food Secure, Black Non-Hispanic, Female, Age 26, 2-person household

Networks

Kin are a vital coping strategy for households who experience a shortfall in resources for food. The most common assistance offered is frequent invitations to meals. Toward the end of the month, several needy households ate most of their meals at relatives' homes. Kin might also drop by with a couple of bags of groceries, or even offer cash, though this is less common. A casual meal invitation—or two, or three, or more—or a surprise "visit" in which "extra" groceries are bestowed relieves embarrassment; even needy households often try to take pride in their independence and find the receipt of "charity" demeaning.

One respondent explained how her parents' penchant for extending meal invitations or just "stopping by" saves her from the embarrassment of asking for help. "My mom and dad live close by. So, I don't like to let them know [when I've run out of money for food]. But if they're aware, if I happen to mention something, my dad will be like, "Come on over for dinner or something!" Or they'll stop by [and say], "Oh, I bought some extra!" even though I know they didn't buy extra."[55] Another told a similar story of how his family helps him out: "The beautiful thing about that is I have family, you know what I mean? I have family. We're a tight-knit family and her family's a tight-knit family…. They'll give me cash or they'll say, 'Well, I'm making spaghetti, why don't you all come over here and eat? We're cooking out; we got the grill going on. Why don't you all come over and eat?' So you know what I mean?"[56]

Claiming kin support is not without its costs. Some respondents report feeling considerable shame when relatives do not "offer" help and the respondents must ask for it. One respondent put it this way: "I go to my mom's. I crawl back to my mom like a little baby. And I tell mom, I be like, 'Momma, I need help.' She'll be like, 'Well, I'll see what I can do for you.'"[57] Another shared the embarrassment she experiences when she asks her mother for food,

> "Oh my God. The last time [I had to beg] was probably about a month and a half ago that I really didn't have anything [to buy food with].
>
> (Interviewer: And what did you do?)
>
> I went to my mother's house and said "Mom, I really don't have anything to eat," and she gave me a bag of rice, beans, and meats for the whole week. She's - obviously - she tries right now to help me out a lot. It's just hard, and it's a little bit embarrassing to go through that."[58]

Some respondents have network resources that can be reliably drawn upon month after month. Often, these households are drawing on kin who are better off than they are. Others' networks are not as reliable, often because the kin in their network are in unstable situations or in similar straits. One respondent in the latter group told us,

---

[55] P2: Low Food Security, Hispanic, Female, Age 45, 3-person household

[56] P65: Food Secure, Black Non-Hispanic, Male, Age 42, 3-person household

[57] P69: Food Secure, Black Non-Hispanic, Female, Age 19, 2-person household

[58] P57: Low Food Security, Hispanic, Female, Age 42, 6-person household

"It's just really like the last year and a half that I've been struggling a lot because my ex-father-in-law, which is my husband's father, used to help me out a lot.

(Interviewer: He used to help you?)

Yeah, he would bring food and stuff for the kids. But he's been sick also, so it's been a while since he hasn't been able to provide for me in the way that he used to provide for me and the kids."[59]

Some say their kin simply tire of helping, especially when implicit norms of reciprocity cannot be met. A respondent in this situation says,

"I've lost a lot of friends in the last few years; people that you borrow from but you can't pay back.

(Interviewer: So when people - they employ other strategies. They go to friend's house or a relative's house.)

I don't have any of that [any more]."[60]

Like the above respondent, a significant number of respondents specifically state that they are bereft of network resources. One respondent describes her situation as follows:

"Really as far as relatives, since my Mom died, they just pushed me to the curb…. I got an auntie that used to only be around the corner—she act like she hated me when my mama died. My uncles—my mother's brothers—they stay on the south side. They don't call. They know I'm sick and I got these kids, they don't call and see if I'm all right, if I need anything. But when my mom was living they brought my mom food, extra food and clothes for the kids and helped her out."[61]

We asked one mother, who claimed she had no network resources, "Tell me how you deal when [food] money gets tight?" She replied, "I cry. I cry and I pray and I try to find people to beg from. It's like 'Oh my God, I don't know.' I try to find somebody that might need me to do something for them so they can pay me."[62] Another respondent told us about a time when she experienced food hardship and had no one to turn to for help:

"When I completely ran out of food, I was hurting really bad.

(Interviewer: Was it a few months ago or?)

Yes.

---

[59] P57: Low Food Security, Hispanic, Female, Age 42, 6-person household

[60] P12: Very Low Food Security, Other, Male, Age 57, 3-person household

[61] P55: Very Low Food Security, Black Non-Hispanic, Female, Age 40, 8-person household

[62] P4: Very Low Food Security, White Non-Hispanic, Female, Age 35, 6-person household

(Interviewer: Okay. Can you tell me that whole story from start to finish?)

When I ran out one time I didn't have - I don't think I had really nothing. Water I don't care you can drink that and whatever but we had run out of food. I think at the time somebody was out of town I don't remember who it was I forgot, I was calling around trying to get money and stuff. I had enough to feed him his hotdogs and stuff but he had run out of that because it was only two in the pack. I was calling, I even tried to call his father and he said he didn't have no money and stuff so that time I had a real tough but he didn't go starving…. It was enough in his belly for where he could wait until the next day….

(Interviewer: How did you cope with that?)

It's kind of hurtful, painful to go through that knowing you have nothing and whatever."[63]

The food secure are more likely than families with lower food security—36 percent versus 24 for the low and 22 for the very low food secure—to rely on kin for shared meals, groceries, or cash for food. But there are differences in the kind of kin assistance that families with food security receive as well. The network resources of the food secure typically offer a *regular* source of food assistance that can be *relied* upon each month, and the network members the food secure draw upon are often considerably *better off* than they are. For example, one respondent explains how she meets her food expenses by receiving support from both of her grandmothers. One of her grandmothers cooks big meals and invites her over for meals regularly, and her other grandmother takes her out for meals on a regular basis:

"Well usually like I said, my Grandma will take me somewhere to eat and then anything I buy at the grocery store I can use food stamps. But when we go out to eat you can't buy food with food stamps so she will just pay for it."[64]

Those in the very low food security category seldom have access to regular and reliable support. One such respondent tells us,

"Well, there's times I, okay, like, my grandma [who had been helping me out a lot with food] got really sick in March and my mom had to go to Corpus Christi. So if she's not there we're kind of like, what do we do, you know? So that's when either I go to the food bank or I'm trying to figure something out, like, 'What?,' you know?"[65]

As is evident from the quote above, those lower in the food security hierarchy must often draw on kin whose situations are unstable, or who are not much better off than they are even in the best of times. Sharing food across households can ensure that when one household is in the black, they

---

[63] P59: Low Food Security, Black Non-Hispanic, Female, Age 22, 3-person household

[64] P36: Food Secure, White Non-Hispanic, Female, Age 19, 3-person household

[65] P77: Very Low Food Security, White Non-Hispanic, Female, Age 25, 2-person household

can help the household in the red, and everyone benefits. But when everyone in the network is struggling, these arrangements can fall short and lead to food hardship.

Another difference to note is that food secure households are almost always on the receiving, not the giving, end of shared meal arrangements, while a notable minority in the less food secure categories are on the giving end, either because they have had to offer shelter and food to children, grandchildren, or other relatives in need or because they espouse a strong norm of sharing what they have with others who are hungry. As we have noted above, several in this group hold strong moral or religious beliefs about the importance of sharing what resources one has with the needy. Their networks may also be different from those of the food secure; perhaps the reason they are more likely to give is that they have more needy network members who call on them for assistance. For instance, one respondent explained that her uncle and his wife recently moved in with her family, creating more difficulty in providing enough food for everyone. She explains,

> "Well right now since you asked, we have a relative right now living with us. My uncle and his wife, they're living with us right now since November of last year because - so since then, sometimes we do struggle more than before. So we struggle a little more but not as much - well, we do…[We] try to eat the same thing to everybody but since sometimes right now, like my uncle - his wife is kind of a meat eater so every time she wants to eat meat. Meat, meat, every day so if we don't have – it's too bad. You know, you have to eat what we have. Sometimes she's like, 'Oh, I don't want to eat. I don't want this. I don't want that.' I'm sorry, we don't have any so…"[66]

Food Pantries

A little more than a third (36 percent) of families use food pantries to cope with food hardship. There were not large differences in the propensity to use food pantries by food security level. Respondents almost uniformly view this strategy as a last resort. One common complaint is that the food is often past its expiration date and quickly spoils, becoming unusable. Another is that the type of items provided are sometimes not what a respondent is used to cooking with, or what the children are willing to consume. The most common reason respondents avoid food pantries is that they feel others are more in need, and they should leave the resources available at food pantries to those who have nothing to eat. This sentiment, while charitable, seems to also reflect the high degree of stigma respondents feel when they approach a food pantry for assistance.

One respondent describes her experience at a food bank, where the food was expired and rotten, and she decided not to return after that experience:

> "I used a food bank but we basically - that food bank that we went to is almost the things that were given us, it was already expired…So it's also the bread. The vegetables just past. It was just -…It was like 2 years ago. I just went for a couple of times. I didn't go for the whole year. Just went for a couple of times since I started to go and I seen when I got the stuff - I seen this when I get home. I had seen that this was already expired for a week, 2 weeks before…So, yeah. I stopped going.

---

[66] P15: Low Food Security, Hispanic, Female, Age 29, 6-person household

(Interviewer: And how did you learn about that place? How did you learn about the food bank? You don't remember?)

No. No, not really because the most of the banks that we have that were given us, it was just something that we don't know what to do because really it's something that they've given us that is not edible....It was not eatable. It was just like put it away, don't eat it because it's already expired or even the vegetables. They were already -

(Interviewer: Starting to rot?)

Yeah."[67]

When asked if she has ever gone to a food pantry, another respondent explains her view of food pantries, "No because that would be greedy if I can get it other ways like from my mom. That's greedy. There are other people that need it."[68]

One respondent shares that she does go to food pantries occasionally, but finds it embarrassing:

"A few times I've had to go to where they do like a church kind of thing and they. . .

(Interviewer: Like a food pantry at the church?)

Yeah, kind of like a pantry thing. Yeah. So I've gone there, probably two or three times. I don't like to.

(Interviewer: Why? Why don't you like to?)

I don't know...I think it's embarrassing."[69]

Careful Meal Planning

As noted in the introduction to this chapter, we looked at the food coping strategies of all respondents, not just those who reported a financial shortfall related to food in a recent month. When faced with a tight food budget, a highly effective proactive strategy is to engage in an elaborate set of techniques to save money on food. While nearly everyone in this sample clips coupons and comparison shops, these individuals shop often, and at many stores, to get the best deals. They also carefully plan meals around sales, and make sure to stick to a grocery list and to avoid impulse buying, even if an item is on sale. About one in five (19 percent) of households reported this type of strategy. But whereas more than a quarter of the more food secure do so (27 percent of the food secure and 28 percent of the low food secure), only 8 percent of those who have very low food security do so.

Many of our respondents are consummate bargain hunters when it comes to food. The most savvy often visit three of four different stores on a regular basis to secure the best bargains, buy

---

[67] P15: Low Food Security, Hispanic, Female, Age 29, 6-person household

[68] P16: Low Food Security, Black Non-Hispanic, Female, Age 37, 3-person household

[69] P2: Low Food Security, Hispanic, Female, Age 45, 3-person household

nothing that is not on sale, and buy in bulk when they can (if they have adequate storage space). Here is an example of how one respondent executes this strategy with skill:

"(Interviewer: Okay, so let's talk more about what you spend on food, starting with April, the last 30 days. Take me through the month starting with your biggest grocery shopping and what you spent.)

Well, since right now I am struggling, I am trying to work as much as I can with whatever they send me. So I try to limit myself to $125 or $150 a week; which is very little, right? I try to use every single thing. Before, we used to throw out lettuce and peppers, you know, that stuff. Now, I try to use every single bit. My refrigerator is empty sometimes but that's because I'm using everything wisely. It's because I'm putting effort into it, you know? So I look at all the papers to see which ones have the most sales; I make a list of the stuff that I need and want, and then just go one day and hit the stores and buy the stuff. It's just the stuff I have on my list. And I try to eat before I go to the store, because if you go to the store and you're hungry it's like you just need to pick up whatever.

(Interviewer: Do you ever find that you put something in your cart and then you find yourself taking it back out later?)

I used to do that but not anymore. I used to do that a lot because I was tempted to buy chips and cookies and stuff for the kids and I was like 'Oh, I can't have this; they don't really need this.'

(Interviewer: What's interesting about this is you basically use the food stamps to set up a limit. I'm not going to spend - it doesn't sound like you spend one more penny on food [than you have to]).

No, I can't."[70]

Another describes her shopping strategy as follows:

"(Interviewer: So how much are you getting from SNAP right now?)

$274.

(Interviewer: $274. And then do you - tell me if you pay more than that for food each month).

No, I'm very frugal and I use coupons and I use menus. I make menus so that if I buy a meat, I can at least use it for 2 meals and I cook it and use it for 2 meals in a row. I buy vegetables that are on sale, you know. Usually frozen ones are on sale so that's what I do. I worked in the accounting department [before I lost my job.] That's how I do this, you know? Because it helps. My sister taught me that, the menu

---

[70] P57: Low Food Security, Hispanic, Female, Age 42, 6-person household

and stick to the menu and you'll be fine. Yeah. Like I said, I look to see what's on sale; I plan a menu around that."[71]

To stave off food hardship, particularly toward the end of the month, many devise ingenious strategies for making food "stretch," such as cooking large quantities of spaghetti, potatoes, or other relatively cheap starches that can last several days or by adding vegetables or meat to Top Ramen to make a "cheap but healthy" meal. We learned about many different "Ramen plus" recipes.

A sizeable minority—more than a quarter—of those in the more food secure groups make food shopping a part-time job, and take considerable pride in their savings. These strategies include taking inventory of what is in the cupboards before going shopping, making a list of what to buy at the store and sticking to it, planning the exact meals they will make during the week or month and purchasing the ingredients only for those meals, buying in bulk when items are on sale, searching for sales, and going to multiple stores to get the best deals. These strategies likely reflect discipline and skill as well as the fact that, on average, these respondents' overall financial situations are somewhat more stable than those with lower levels of food security. One food secure respondent explains that she used to have trouble sticking to a budget when shopping, but has learned now to make a list and to only buy things on that list when grocery shopping:

> "Yeah. Well, I'll take the list and this is, uh, I'll take the list and, "Okay, I'm going to spend $120." And I'll go to a store and it's like, 'Oh, these are on sale. I'm just going to get these because they're on sale' or we need them. And the budget kind of goes out the window. So, like, I'm better now at applying it, you know. If I go to the supermarket with a list I stick to it. And it doesn't matter if we don't, we didn't get something that's on the list, we'll make do. We have to."[72]

Another respondent spends a lot of time planning meals based on coupons. He gathers coupons to see what is on sale, makes a menu based off of the coupons, and then purchases only the food that will fill out his planned menu. He explains his shopping strategy,

> "Some people buy - like me, I'll buy chicken breasts but the skinless is a little more because they have to take the skin. Well, which is more healthy for you, you know what I mean? So it depends on where I'm at as far as the refrigerator is concerned. If the refrigerator is full - well, not full but you know, full of - all right, we have chicken, we have this, we have that, so let's get something that we don't normally get, you know, because every week, like I said, sometimes I'll buy a week's worth of groceries, you know what I mean, and I buy dinners. I don't go in there and just buy groceries. I say, 'Okay, we're going to have...'

> (Interviewer: Plan a menu.)

> Exactly.

> (Interviewer: So you go to grocery shop with a list and a bunch of coupons?)

---

[71] P66: Low Food Security, Hispanic, Female, Age 64, 2-person household

[72] P17: Food Secure, Black Non-Hispanic, Female, Age 33, 2-person household

Absolutely and you know, we can have spaghetti. I make a big pot of spaghetti. That's 2 days.

(Interviewer: Right. Yeah. So you know what you're doing. You really -)

You gotta make it work. You gotta make it work and I stay away from, you know - even though it's buy one get one free with the potato chips, you know, we don't do that."[73]

Although some respondents in the very low food security group do engage in meal planning efforts, overall the strategies of those in the very low food security group are more likely to be haphazard, as this quote shows:

"It's kind of spur of the moment. There is no real plan because by the time you make a list you go in the store and half the stuff is overpriced so I'm not going to buy it anyway."[74]

D. Chapter III Summary

Unforeseen disruptions to income or benefits, or some necessary extra expenditure can upset the delicate balance these families strike on a monthly basis to put food on the table for their children. Families across America see ebbs and flows in their finances from month to month, but families receiving SNAP benefits typically have far less ability to absorb the financial shock of an illness, extra holiday expenses, a costly medical prescription, or a cutback in hours at work.

Income and government benefits are not the sole determining factor of a family's food security; even among the food secure, the food budget is typically very tight. Even the food secure respondents in this study reported that they can rarely get by without deploying specific strategies to stretch their food resources. Regularly restricting food intake toward the end of the month to get by is common even among those families we interviewed who were food secure; generally this means that the adults in the household must regularly skip meals. In fact, skipping meals is so common, and many of these adults in the study, including those who are food secure by our survey measure, have skipped meals so often and for such a long time, that it is not described as anything out of the ordinary; in fact, it is seldom even conceived of as a hardship. Also quite striking is the fact that those in all food security level groups in this study say that the type of food they consume changes dramatically toward the end of the month.

Although the sample was too small to warrant making claims about differences in food hardship and coping patterns that distinguish food secure households from low and very low food security households, we do note several striking patterns in the data. Based on these patterns, we venture three hypotheses in this regard.

First, much is determined by the resources that families have to draw on outside their income and government benefits. While many families find their refrigerators growing empty toward the end

---

[73] P65: Food Secure, Black Non-Hispanic, Male, Age 42, 3-person household

[74] P12: Very Low Food Security, Other, Male, Age 57, 3-person household

of the month, having a network of family or friends to turn to when faced with these situations often makes the difference in being food secure. A sizeable minority of the food secure in this study say they eat meals at the homes of family members and friends to stretch food resources, or share responsibilities for providing groceries and engaging in meal preparation with other households. Fully 36 percent do so, or garner groceries, or borrow cash for food from kin. In contrast, families with very low food security often say that they have nowhere to turn when there is nothing left; they have either exhausted their networks or lack them entirely. Some of these families regularly stretch their resources to help others in their networks who are less fortunate.

Second, low, and especially very low food security families are more likely to be subject to problems with SNAP recertification and abrupt drops in other government benefits, which causes them to experience dramatic dips in their resources. Households typically carefully construct their budgets around the expectation that they can cover most, if not all, of their food expenses with SNAP. Thus, the loss of SNAP especially, even for a brief period of time, is almost certain to spark food hardship.

Finally, because of a lack of time and resources, the weight of other demands, and/or poor coping skills, households with very low food security are often less able to be proactive in preparing for spells of food hardship in the ways more secure families do: bargain hunting, carefully planning menus around sales, and stockpiling. The patterns in the circumstances and behaviors of very low food security households may reflect deeper instabilities in their familial circumstances or social networks, which may be the root cause of why they are not emulating the strategies of food secure families.

IV. STRATEGIES HOUSEHOLDS USE TO MEET FOOD NEEDS

How do families acquire the food they consume each month? What preferences and constraints guide what lands in the shopping cart and what remains on the grocer's shelf? How do families approach the challenge of acquiring food? When and where do they shop? How frugal are they as food shoppers, and what strategies do they use to make their food dollars last through the end of the month? What do these strategies require in terms of their time, emotional energy, and ingenuity?

This chapter will show that the households in this study expend their SNAP resources almost solely for food. Only one respondent reported trading SNAP for cash or other non-food goods or services. Most steward their SNAP resources with great care, scrimping and saving to make benefits stretch as far as they can. Food is expensive, they say, and despite clipping coupons and visiting a number of stores to get the very best deals they can, few can manage to make their SNAP last through the month. Though for many households SNAP is not designed to cover all of families' food needs[75], respondents often believe it ought to do so. At the end of the month, ensuring adequate food requires devoting a very scarce resource, cash, to food at a time in the month where there is little or no cash to be had.

Despite past experience of lean times at months' end, families only rarely earmark a portion of their cash resources for food. When SNAP benefits are expended, they are often left scrambling. Likewise, in the absence of SNAP, many families say that in order to meet other pressing financial obligations such as rent and utilities, they cannot protect enough of their cash income from these demands to ensure an adequate supply of food.[76] This is despite the fact that nearly all of the families in this study say they prioritize food when making financial tradeoffs. For example, a family that suddenly loses SNAP might be willing to risk a utility shut off so they can spend more of their cash for food, but they might be more hesitant to skip a rent payment and risk eviction.

In this chapter, we discuss where respondents do their grocery shopping, the types of food they buy, the preferences and constraints that guide their choices, and their strategies for stretching their food dollars. Chicken, hamburger, pork, and occasionally fish top the list of items a household feels it must purchase each month. Many buy fresh fruit, but often choose frozen over fresh vegetables in the absence of an especially good bargain. Almost all buy large quantities of nonperishables: staples such as rice, pasta and beans; canned goods; and prepackaged foods and snacks. Most also purchase a variety of juices and sodas and occasionally bottled water.

---

[75] The value of the SNAP benefit is set each year based on the cost of the Thrifty Food Plan (TFP) for a family of four in June of the prior year, with adjustments for household size and geographic area (if outside of the Continental United States). SNAP benefit amounts are computed on the basis of a household's net monthly income, the benefit reduction rate, and the maximum SNAP benefit for its household size and location. A household's monthly SNAP benefit is computed by subtracting 30 percent of its net income from the maximum benefit. If a household has zero net income (that is, its deductible expenses equal or exceed its gross income), it receives the maximum SNAP benefit. As specified in the Food and Nutrition Act of 2008, as amended, the maximum benefit was 113.6 percent of the June 2008 TFP in fiscal year 2010 (Eslami et al. 2011). Thus, the benefit level is designed to cover all food expenditures only for households with approximaely zero net income. In an average month in fiscal year 2010, 32.4 percent of households with children received the maximum benefit (Eslami et al. 2011, Table A.12).

[76] The exception is in late winter and early spring, when many receive substantial lump sums from refundable tax credits such as the EITC.

To stretch their food dollars further, household heads scour newspapers, grocery store circulars and internet offers, comparing prices and clipping coupons to ensure the very best deals. Many travel to two, and often three or four, different stores to get the best bargains, and the especially savvy may do so several times each month. Some have to travel outside their immediate neighborhoods for the lowest prices, and must sometimes take several buses or hitch a ride with a friend to get back and forth to each store. These strategies are routinely practiced across all food security categories, but they are practiced to a lesser degree among the least food secure.

A. Number and Type of Stores/Frequency of Grocery Shopping

Many respondents rely on a single large chain supermarket for most of their groceries. This is not necessarily the supermarket nearby; when possible, respondents typically eschew more expensive local stores for retailers that can be counted upon to offer better bargains, even if they are some distance away. Most respondents seem well informed about the merits and disadvantages of each grocery store and food retailer in the area, including which accept SNAP. Proximity and accessibility are nonetheless factors in deciding where to shop. One respondent said that one of the reasons she shopped the Ralph's Supermarket in her Los Angeles neighborhood was that it offered a shuttle, and even a ride home if one spent more than $25.[77]

In addition to their main store, almost all visit additional stores offering especially steep discounts on specific items they feel they can use. Some visit meat markets to purchase their meat, largely because the prices are lower than at the supermarket. We asked one participant, "So each week you wait for the flyers to come out, and then you see what is on sale, and then you go to those stores to buy things?"

> "Most of the time I purchase produce at the Korean market. Or sometimes even some Mexican stores. Just meat I purchase the items that are on sale. For example, fruit like this I bought two for $1.00 at Ralph's then I found out a Korean market had some five pieces for $1.00. So that is the way I spend money, produce I just look at flyers. Every week different store have products on sale so I purchase the items on sale."[78]

When asked whether they shopped at the "dollar" store, many respondents replied in the affirmative but then revealed that they usually bought only cleaning supplies and other non-food items there. One respondent, however, provided a long list of all the fresh produce available at her local dollar store. Others find the prices on frozen snacks, such as mini-pizzas, cheaper there.

Most respondents do the majority of their grocery shopping when their SNAP benefit arrives, but some carefully apportion their SNAP so they can make several smaller trips. Purchases of meat, fruit, and fresh vegetables, as well as milk and bread, require several monthly trips, while staples and frozen goods are usually purchased at the beginning of the month. Meat and fresh produce are often the most expensive items on the grocery lists, and respondents must often travel to several stores to maximize savings on these items. We asked one respondent, "[You've talked about Jo Bees and Kroger—specials at Kroger's. Any other stores that you go to other than those two?" She replied,

---

[77] P25: Low Food Security, Black Non-Hispanic, Female, Age 43, 4-person household

[78] P24: Very Low Food Security, Other, Female, Age 57, 3-person household

"Wal-Mart or Family Dollar…if there is a special. If it's on sale…. I only go to Wal-Mart for food when it's something on sale. Like if I see in the sales paper they have a lot of fruit, some blackberries or something on sale and…it's cheaper at Wal-Mart I'll go to Wal-Mart."[79]

As should be evident from the narrative above, the process of acquiring food is one that requires considerable time and ingenuity. Because the food budget is generally tight, and the stakes high—they feel it is imperative that their children do not go without—it can also be the source of considerable stress.

B. Types of Foods Purchased

This section describes what goes into the grocery cart, as well as the preferences and constraints that guide what families put in the cart or leave on the shelf. Level of food security is not strongly associated with the types of foods that respondents purchase. Those with very low food security shop at the same grocery stores and buy more-or-less similar products as those who are more food secure. But as noted above, their grocery carts often contain less variety than those of households with more food security. In contrast, the food secure are somewhat more likely than those with less food security to indulge in items they consider "treats" when they shop (e.g., cream cheese, Craisins, mangos, or ready-made cake).

Snacks

Respondents often place strong emphasis on the importance of purchasing snacks that their children can consume between lunch and dinner. These comprise mostly dessert-like items such as cookies, mini-donuts, honey buns, and snack cakes, or items such as mini-pizzas and other premade frozen snacks. Respondents list snacks, along with more nutritious items, as a vital component of their grocery baskets. They do so in a matter-of-fact way, perhaps indicating that they worry less about the nutritional value of snacks than they do when it comes to what goes on the table at mealtimes. In sum, while many think carefully about how to prepare balanced and nutritious lunches and dinners for their children, not many are thinking about how to make their children's between-meal snacks healthier. One respondent, for example, said:

> "I buy the jellos because they're only a dollar for a pack of four. So I buy a lot of those, because the baby eats them. I sent them to school for her snack, and they like eating those. You know, it's okay. Kids deserve snacks and I feel jello and pudding is not that bad of a snack."[80]

Several respondents, though, were careful to limit the amount of junk food in their grocery carts. We asked all respondents, "Is there anything that you put in your cart and take out later?" One replied, "Whenever [my daughter] sneaks in junk food. I'm not a big [one to] keep junk food in the house…because junk food isn't going to do anything for you except accept make you hyper and drive you crazy, so we try to keep the junk food out of the cart."[81]

---

[79] P16: Low Food Security, Black Non-Hispanic, Female, Age 37, 3-person household

[80] P6: Food Secure, Black Non-Hispanic, Female, Age 28, 4-person household

[81] P18: Very Low Food Security, Hispanic, Female, Age 38, 4-person household

Pre-prepared Foods

Respondents buy large quantities and a large variety of pre-prepared foods. These include fish sticks, chicken nuggets, and chicken fingers. A large number of respondents also buy "Lunchables" for their children's lunch on occasion. Hamburger Helper and Rice-A-Roni make frequent appearances at the dinner table, as do frozen pizza, potpies, instant macaroni and cheese, and canned soup. Frozen pizza is particularly common. As noted above, a lot of snacks are also pre-prepared, such as frozen burritos, hot pockets, and corn dogs. Among those in this sample, Hispanic families reported purchasing somewhat fewer pre-prepared foods for dinner than other racial/ethnic groups.

Beverages

Respondents frequently purchase Kool-Aid Fruit, Clifford, Capri Sun, and other individual-serving juice products, though some try to buy products that are lower in sugar or higher in nutritional content (e.g., V8). Some respondents who also buy soda; some, but not all, acknowledge that soda is not healthful. Families rarely serve water from the tap at home or serve water as a beverage at meals. One respondent with very low food security said:

> "We load up on juice because I hate to run out of stuff to drink. I know there is still water but I make sure I drink water all day at work, over and over. When I'm home and I'm eating, I want something else, so we load up on juice for the month so we don't run out."[82]

When respondents drink water, it is usually bottled. Thus, for our respondents, then, the choice might actually be not between free water and expensive juice, but between expensive water and expensive juice. Perhaps respondents simply prefer a beverage with some flavor at a meal.

Fruits and Vegetables

Many respondents say their children like fruit, and make sure to pick up several different types of fruit in the produce aisle. Fruit can be substituted for less healthy items as a snack or eaten as part of the lunch or dinner meal. Fresh vegetable purchases are far less frequent. Respondents often say they fear that fresh vegetables will spoil before they can be used, so they do not view such purchases as economical unless a particularly good bargain can be had. Even then, they go to the frozen foods aisle for the rest, or buy canned vegetables. We asked one respondent, "Is there anything that you want to buy that you just can't afford?"

> "Probably like the fresh vegetables. We like to eat those but I usually go to the canned good aisle and get the canned goods. They're a little cheaper than the fresh vegetables because they last longer than the fresh vegetables."[83]

Within this sample, those with very low food security typically buy the fewest fresh vegetables and limit themselves to basic salad components or ingredients for sandwiches, like lettuce, tomatoes,

---

[82] P41: Very Low Food Security, Black Non-Hispanic, Female, Age 23, 2-person household

[83] P14: Food Secure, White Non-Hispanic, Female, Age 30, 3-person household

and onions, and perhaps some potatoes. Some with very low food security say they are unable to purchase any fresh produce. One such respondent said that she and her family are unable to afford "meals"—meaning balanced lunches and dinners—because fruit and vegetables are entirely out of her price range. We asked, "Is there anything that you want to buy that you just can't afford, in the grocery store?"

> "…we're thankful for the $200 [from SNAP] but it just doesn't seem like enough…to have a meal every day. If we did try a meal for every day, or try to cook [all three meals—], breakfast, lunch, dinner—it wouldn't be enough money. And to get fruits and stuff that we should be getting, especially for my daughter, and salad and all that stuff, that stuff is too expensive; we can't even look at it….

> (Interviewer: And the fruits and vegetables at Joe V's [discount grocery story], are they affordable or no?)

> They're a little cheaper but apples are still expensive. We would have to put [other] food back to get fruits and vegetables. Then we would run out of food. So we don't even look that way; we don't get them even though we should be getting them.

> (Interviewer: It's a problem when produce is more expensive than other things.)

> Really, the healthier food period is more expensive. The stuff that we should get that is good for us, we probably can't get it."[84]

C. Approaches to Grocery Shopping

We asked respondents how they decided what to buy and what not to buy when grocery shopping. Price is their primary consideration. Nutrition, while a concern, often takes a distant second place. Many in the very low food security category explicitly said they could not afford to eat healthfully. One respondent, when asked how she decided what to buy or what not to buy, said,

> "Depending on price usually, yeah, price is such a big factor. If I'm getting [only] this much for $6.00 is it really worth it? Is this going to feed everybody or should I look for something a little cheaper, a little bigger? Price has a lot to do with it. Price and [then] quantity."[85]

Many respondents plan meals and create detailed meal plans and shopping lists before visiting a store, deciding where to buy what after researching newspaper ads and circulars for sales. One keeps a mental list of the food groups in her head and scours store circulars to find a deal for items in each group. We asked her, "How do you decide where you're going to go on your shopping trips? What's your method on deciding?"

> "I figure out what I want to eat for that week—really two weeks at a time. [In my] meal planning I'll…decide, well, I'm going to be eating a lot of rice, regular rice, so

---

[84] P41: Very Low Food Security, Black Non-Hispanic, Female, Age 23, 2-person household

[85] P18: Very Low Food Security, Hispanic, Female, Age 38, 4-person household

BJ's has the best price on rice so I'll go buy the rice there and I'm going to get their potatoes because they have the 20lb bags versus the 5lb bags. So basically it revolves around meal planning.

(Interviewer: That makes sense.)

And then from there I'll decide, 'Okay, who has sales on meat?' and so on and so forth and that's how I'll do it."[86]

A careful accounting of what remains in the cupboard—what items have been expended or are running low—lays the groundwork for grocery list preparation. One respondent explains, "I always check my cupboards to see what I need and what I don't need and done. I always check before I go because I don't buy anything that's unnecessary."[87]

Households may shop for groceries every week, or even several times a week, so they can take advantage of discounts within the time frames for which they are available. Shopping frequently to capitalize fully on sales incurs additional transportation costs and takes time, but these shoppers believe the savings outweighs these costs. One told us,

> "I wait till the sales come out which is usually on Wednesday or Tuesday and on the following day I will find out what is on sale. If chicken breast is on sale and they are on sale for $1.29 then I will get the limit and even go back the next day and get [more]. I get it, separate it, freeze it and so we have several nights. If [it's] pork shoulder they have...on sale..., if you get a double pack it is $12.00, but it is two...meals [in] each [pack]. You can make burritos or whatever with it one day and then put it over rice [the next]. So that is how I shop by the sales ads, strictly by the sales ads."[88]

Some respondents carry a calculator with them during shopping trips, or use the calculator feature on their cell phones to tally their bill as they shop. Others keep a mental running tally. Despite their best efforts to plan meals and keep within a budget, they must often return items to the shelves or set them aside at checkout. Some respondents place items on the conveyor belt in order of necessity and then watch the tally. This way, they can simply leave any items they cannot afford in the grocery cart rather than having to make that determination after their SNAP card has already been declined. Having one's card declined is repeatedly cited as a source of great embarrassment. One respondent described how she felt the last time this happened.

> "It is awful embarrassing getting up there and then the card is denied. When they deny it they go, 'Mister, your card is denied!' as loud as they can. Last time the lady did that I looked right at her and said, 'Can you say it any louder?' So she pushed the button for the manager to come over and he says, 'What's the problem?' I said 'Well,

---

[86] P7: Very Low Food Security, White Non-Hispanic, Female, Age 41, 4-person household

[87] P32: Low Food Security, Hispanic, Female, Age 24, 4-person household

[88] P1: Low Food Security, White Non-Hispanic, Female, Age 47, 3-person household

my card doesn't cover it so I can't buy all of it and your teller has a loud mouth.' And then I asked the manager if he could please help me sort it out. He did."[89]

The majority of respondents say they must sacrifice quality in order to purchase enough food to get through the month. One follows specific rules with regard to what cuts of meat he allows himself to buy. We asked him, "So in general, how do you decide what to buy and what not to buy?" "Prices, and you know meat, chicken, I can't buy breasts, only legs and thighs," he tells us.[90]

Several respondents say that they save on food costs by cooking the same meals each week, and do not add any ingredients that are not strictly necessary, sometimes sacrificing flavor. Shoppers who deploy this strategy rarely try anything new. We asked whether there was anything she wanted to buy that she just couldn't afford, and one respondent said,

> "Uh, just extra ingredients. Sometimes that you think that you might want to try something different and we just know we can't get it because you need so many ingredients for one meal that it's just no point. Just cook what you know and that's it.
>
> (Interviewer: Yeah. That's tough. I do that, too. I want to - yeah, you have a special spice or something-)
>
> Right…. It's like, really if I get that spice then I need this spice and… Yeah. I'll just stick to what I know and it's very generic."[91]

This quote illustrates just how closely most respondents stick to their grocery lists, and how little flexibility they have. Most stick to a strict budget as well. We asked one respondent, "Let's say that we are at Market Basket, [where you said you do your big grocery shopping trip], and you have your cart - where will we go first?"

> "First I go to the aisle where the dairy [is, and buy] mozzarella cheese, orange juice, 1% low-fat milk. I walk up to the eggs and I grab a dozen or a dozen and a half…and then I go to the dry food aisle and get corn meal, sugar, cooking oil, rice, canned beans to cook pupusas, dried beans for me, chocolate, a can of coffee for the month. Then I walk over to the meat section and get a can of meat, one or two chickens, one or two packages of wings and thighs, liver, chicken gizzards. Sometimes I get fish—salmon, tilapia—one or two [and] depending on the price…, a package of pork meat. After that I go to the vegetable section and get lettuce, tomatoes, green chili peppers, radishes, pearl onions, beef bones to make soup, cassava, green plantains. I then approach the bread aisle and get the sliced bread, and…then I approach the frozen section and I get green tamales, vegetables for the rice, and sometimes I'm able to get a bag of French fries, lollipops, ice cream for [family member]. If I'm in the mood to make tamales, I get the leaf to make tamales, water, soda, juices. Sometimes when I'm unable to get the soda or juices, I get two

---

[89] P12: Very Low Food Security, Other, Male, Age 57, 3-person household

[90] P9: Very Low Food Security, Black Non-Hispanic, Male, Age 37, 6-person household

[91] P8: Very Low Food Security, Hispanic, Female, Age 32, 3-person household

cans of Kool-Aid in different flavors - that's about it. And then I reach the register and I pay $190, $194; sometimes it comes to exactly the $200.

(Interviewer: So you already know how to shop by heart?)

Yes, I already have my shopping down pat. I don't even pass through certain sections because I won't be able to get anything in those aisles."[92]

Food secure respondents sometimes have some measure of flexibility in their grocery budget. We asked, "So is there anything when you go shopping that you like to buy but you don't buy?"

"Absolutely. Like Cool Whip. Who wouldn't want to have lobsters or who wouldn't want to have some kind of salmon, you know what I mean? Every now and again, depending on what's in the refrigerator, you know—I don't buy lobsters, you know what I mean—but I might buy some salami…, I might buy some salmon or something, you know, as opposed to the filets, the frozen filet, cod filet things, you know? If, depending on how the month went…, if I can afford to do that, I'll do that."[93]

Respondents typically allow health and nutrition concerns to influence their food purchasing only when they feel they can afford to. That said, respondents who have some flexibility with grocery shopping funds are sometimes willing to spend a little extra for healthy food. When we asked one respondent whether she buys juice on a regular basis, she replied, "Yes, we do do some juices, yes. Usually the V8…. That's usually an expense I'm willing to incur, because I try to get the V8 that has a little bit less sugar and a little bit more nutritional value."[94]

Another tells us,

"…I buy some expensive items but it's mostly for the health benefit. That's the way I look at it I'm okay with buying food that's more expensive than you might find as long as it has the added health value for it. I'll buy organic milk which is $6.50 instead of $3.50 a gallon because for me I think that's worth it because I just want to make sure that I'm feeding the kids the healthiest food possible. That's my priority so even if we eat a little bit less food, which we don't just in general, we don't have big appetites anyways so we don't just over eat, we don't eat tons but we…try to eat healthy and rich food. So it's satisfying and we're not feeling hungry afterwards but we're also not eating huge amounts of food. We just want to make sure that we're eating enough that we're staying healthy."[95]

---

[92] P31: Very Low Food Security, Hispanic, Female, Age 30, 2-person household

[93] P65: Food Secure, Black Non-Hispanic, Male, Age 42, 3-person household

[94] P43: Low Food Security, Black Non-Hispanic, Female, Age 54, 2-person household

[95] P63: Low Food Security, White Non-Hispanic, Female, Age 28, 3-person household

D. Chapter IV Summary

SNAP participants are often highly cognizant of how to maximize their benefit each month, and seek a balance between nutrition and variety versus quantity and price. Many have well-developed strategies. Some employ quite elaborate routines to ensure they are getting the best deals on food. Typically this requires shopping at a number of different stores and planning their menu carefully to take full advantage of what is on sale at a particular time. This strategy is the least common among the very low food secure.

While many buy prepared foods, snacks with little nutritional value, and soda or sugary juices, there is a common perception that healthier foods, especially fresh vegetables, are too expensive. Thus, most participants focus on purchasing food that will satisfy their children's desires as cheaply as possible, while explicitly noting that this is not what they would choose if their main goal was to provide a well-balanced diet. This compromise is made to ensure that their SNAP benefits will stretch through as much of the month as possible. Often, a limited food budget requires a diet of little variety and low quality; parents see the key tradeoff as nutrition versus hunger.

V. EATING AND FOOD DYNAMICS WITHIN THE HOUSEHOLD

In the previous chapter, we described how families procured food. Here the focus is on the food they consume. What constitutes a typical breakfast, lunch, and dinner? What about snacks? Does the weekday routine vary on weekends? SNAP aims to put healthy foods into the hands of economically needy households. We ask what SNAP households think unhealthy eating entails, and what respondents think their most unhealthy habits are. We then move to food consumed outside the household. When is food shared across households, when is it not, and why? When do families eat out and why, and what types of venues do they frequent? What health challenges do SNAP households face, and how do these challenges affect their diets? If these families had unlimited food budgets, what types of food do they say they would buy?

Most parents strive to provide healthy food for their families, but patterns of food consumption at lunch, and especially at snack time, are often unhealthy. In fact, parents seem to view snack time as unhealthy almost by definition, and insist on having a reserve of frozen mini-pizzas or sugary snacks on hand in the afternoons. Being able to provide such treats, in fact, seems central to their identities as parents. Yet at mealtime, having children in the home seems to boost parents' commitment to well-balanced meals; when children are away, meals are less carefully planned and less well-balanced. Serious health problems are common among both adults and children and sometimes require special diets, but they are rarely cited as a reason to keep one's diet healthy.

Despite tight budgets, most families do eat out from time to time, or order takeout, for a variety of reasons—to celebrate a special occasion, or because they are pressed for time, for example. Losing SNAP seems to prompt visits to fast-food restaurants, because it is hard to marshal enough cash to conduct a major grocery store run and purchase the numerous items needed for a well-balanced meal. About one in five families routinely eat at the household of family members and friends; most do so at least on occasion. In the prior chapter, we showed that this is a crucial strategy for coping with food hardship, one disproportionately available to the food secure. But our respondents seldom reciprocate, and in fact usually refuse to do so: "I won't feed other people at my kids' expense," one mother said,[96] unless the visitors are children themselves—nieces or nephews or their children's friends. Most hold to the "no entertaining" rule quite fiercely: even on holidays, several respondents sat at home rather than open their doors to family and friends; they simply could not afford to. But on their children's birthdays, they do entertain, often saving for weeks or even months to provide food for the event.

Most households define a healthy diet as one rich in fresh fruits and vegetables, and strive to provide a "real meal"—a vegetable, a starch, and a source of protein—for dinner each night. They named greasy fried food and sugary juices and snacks as the most dangerous culprits in an unhealthy diet. But families consumed a host of such unhealthy items each month, sometimes laying the blame on cultural practices, a child who was a picky eater, or even the desire to offer an occasional trip for ice cream to make their children feel like "ordinary kids." Usually though, good intentions with regard to nutrition were defeated by a single factor: cost. Most claimed it was simply cheaper to eat poorly than to eat well. Notably, pre-prepared foods were seldom identified as unhealthy.

---

[96] P12: Very Low Food Security, Other, Male, Age 57, 3-person household

A. Meals and Snacks at Home

Breakfast is typically a lighter meal during the week than it is over the weekend. Lunch is almost always a simple meal, composed most often of "instant" or ready-to-eat foods, fast food, or leftovers. Dinner is the largest meal of the day—it is usually a balanced meal of meat, starch, and vegetables.

Breakfast

Some adults do not eat any breakfast on weekdays, some eat only cereal, and some eat a full breakfast (bacon and eggs, etc.). Children typically eat breakfast at home; fewer in this sample than expected eat a reduced-price or free breakfast in school (even if they are eligible for it). Cereals vary in nutritional content. They include oatmeal, grits, and sugary cereals like Cocoa Krispies.

On weekends, most respondents eat large breakfasts often composed of eggs and/or pancakes, breakfast meats, and some kind of cereal (usually oatmeal and grits).

Lunch

There is little consistency in what respondents eat for lunch on weekdays. Children typically eat at school or daycare. Adults generally eat leftovers, make something that is quick and easy to prepare (such as instant macaroni or Oodles of Noodles instant soup), or spring for a cheap fast-food meal. We asked one respondent, "…when you eat at work, is that food that you're bringing or buying?" She replied, "That's food that I take. I either take leftovers from the night before or I buy the cups of microwavable macaroni. That's what I've been living off of [for lunch] for the last three months."[97]

On weekends, lunch is again a light meal of something easy to prepare. Several respondents eat lunch at church on Sundays.

Snacks

As noted in the prior chapter, nearly all respondents provide their children an afternoon snack between lunch and dinner. One explained: "They eat…their breakfast and lunches [at school]. As soon as they come in they're practically starving so [I] fix them a sandwich, [or they eat] a Lunchable, a piece fruit, or something. Then I cook about five o'clock. They eat dinner."[98]

Dinner

Dinner is the biggest and most important meal of the day for nearly all respondents, both on weekdays and on weekends. Nearly all have some sort of meat or fish for dinner, though since these are expensive items, ensuring a source of protein is not always possible toward the end of the "month" (the SNAP benefit period). Typically, there is some starch in the meal, usually potatoes or rice. Most also say they make sure to have a vegetable dish (or salad) with the evening meal. As noted in Chapter III, families rely on frozen vegetables more often than fresh, because fresh

---

[97] P44: Low Food Security, White Non-Hispanic, Female, Age 32, 5-person household

[98] P16: Low Food Security, Black Non-Hispanic, Female, Age 37, 3-person household

vegetables spoil too quickly, leading to waste. One respondent explained her dinner planning routine as follows:

> "Dinner is fish and chicken, or we eat - my gosh, he just eats very healthy, he eats a lot of fresh vegetable or frozen vegetables are usually what I purchase. And so a typical meal is usually three courses; it's usually a meat, a vegetable and typically a starch. I went to Costco and I have a huge bag of pinto beans. Thank goodness that we really like those, and so I make chili with those, I make baked beans with those. You know, I've gotten really creative."[99]

Meal Patterns by Food Security Level

Those with very low food security generally eat less-balanced meals, especially at dinner. They are more likely to eat only starches—pasta, ramen noodles, or potatoes—for dinner, particularly toward the end of the month. Heavy reliance on inexpensive starches was a common coping mechanism among households lower in food security.

Some household heads in the very low food security category actively choose to eat only two meals a day because of limited funds, though there are parents in all food security groups who regularly skip meals. Many respondents said they skip meals because they simply cannot afford to eat three meals a day. One respondent explained, "If we eat breakfast, we don't have lunch. If we don't have lunch, yeah, vice versa, because we don't, we don't eat three meals a day. We only eat two."[100] Another said, "And on Saturday...I didn't have any breakfast. You really have to be careful because you have to make this money last a whole month. So you really have to be careful. Sometimes you have to eat a little less just to make sure you get through the month."[101]

Children and How They Affect Meal Patterns

Meal patterns change when the children in the household are away. This can happen during school vacations when children are spending time with relatives. It can also be true for respondents who share custody of children with former spouses or partners. Their meals become smaller, more basic, and less balanced when their children are not present. Some parents told us they skip meals altogether when their children are not at home. We asked one respondent, "So what's a typical weekend a typical Saturday or Sunday?" She told us,

> "Well they're actually with their father during the afternoon [on those days] so usually we'll have a breakfast like I said sometimes we'll eat some types of whole grains for breakfast like the oatmeal or quinoa or something.... I'll just kind of get anything to eat—some small meal—to eat for lunch and dinner...."[102]

---

[99] P43: Low Food Security, Black Non-Hispanic, Female, Age 54, 2-person household

[100] P8: Very Low Food Security, Hispanic, Female, Age 32, 3-person household

[101] P70: Very Low Food Security, White Non-Hispanic, Female, Age 54, 2-person household

[102] P63: Low Food Security, White Non-Hispanic, Female, Age 28, 3-person household

Health Issues and How They Affect Meal Patterns

Diabetes, asthma, and food allergies are the most commonly cited health issues our respondents face. They suffer from a variety of food allergies as well, including allergies to dairy, nuts, corn, seafood, eggs, citric acid, chili peppers, and grapefruit. The majority of these allergies did not appear to have been formally diagnosed. However, many respondents gave concrete examples of the kinds of physical reactions they (or their family members) suffered after eating these foods. Both adults and children suffered from food allergies. With a few exceptions, those who required special diets, or had household members who did, made some changes to their diet. Many though had considerable trouble making all the adjustments they felt they needed to, in part because purchasing for more than one kind of diet was expensive. For example, we asked one respondent with diabetes "Does the fact that you have diabetes affect the way you have to shop for food?"

> "I buy [most of what I buy] because of the kids. [But] then I can't cook [the] food [I need]. I haven't learned how to make mine separate from everybody else because it's so many against one. So I try to eat a little less. [The] only time I eat a lot [now] is when I'm mad or I can't resolve a problem that's going on. I solve the problem then I just [go back to just eating less], like before."[103]

B. Eating Out/Ordering Takeout

Respondents usually spend between $20 and $100 each month on eating out or (much less commonly) ordering takeout. While a few respondents say they never eat out, most report doing so roughly once a week, usually at a fast-food restaurant like McDonald's, Taco Bell, or Subway. The McDonald's $1 menu is a particular draw. Those who are food secure occasionally eat out at slightly more expensive restaurants like Applebee's, T.G.I. Friday's, or Olive Garden, though for most, eating at such places is a rare treat rather than a common occurrence.

Respondents usually eat out either to save time when they are pressed for it, to offer a child a treat, to get a change of scenery, or to celebrate a special accomplishment. But loss of SNAP can also trigger trips for fast food.

One respondent described the most recent time her family ate out: "We just went out this past weekend because my daughter, she got her progress report, so she's doing good in school. She wanted to go to Olive Garden. That's where we took her."[104] Another told us,

> "My daughter loves to go to IHOP because she likes pancakes and I don't make pancakes at home. [E]very other Friday—like when I work the weekends I'm off that Friday so my Fridays off—I keep her home [from daycare] with me. So we'll go to IHOP…. She'll say, 'Mommy, do you have money today? Can we go for pancakes?' [It's] not that expensive. Even if I can't eat for myself but I try to treat her, you know what I mean? Because I know she looks forward to it. So I always take her, find a way to $5 or $10 to pay for that.

---

[103] P55: Very Low Food Security, Black Non-Hispanic, Female, Age 40, 8-person household

[104] P20: Low Food Security, Hispanic, Female, Age 23, 4-person household

(Interviewer: Yeah. They give you such giant pancakes and you can probably split it.)

Usually. I mean, I don't ever go out to eat myself to be honest with you but even if I couldn't [take her, I would feel bad]. Like I would make sure that she [gets to go] because she looks forward to it, you know?"[105]

Some respondents say they go out to eat just for a change. "I believe you have to go out once in awhile. You can't be cooped up in the house all the time. Even if it hurts a little you just got to get up and go," one man told us.[106] Another explained,

"We try to go out at least - I have my daughter every other weekend so I'll try to go out at least once a month, you know what I mean…?

(Interviewer: That's nice.)

I like that she's four. I like to take her out now and get her experienced so that by the time she's 10 and 12, when she goes out…she knows how to act and conduct herself when she's out, you know what I mean? And more importantly, why not? You know what I mean? Why not work hard, you know what I mean [so you can do something special with your kids]? I do my carpentry stuff, you know, and I sacrifice my body for my money so I can afford to take my kids out to a Friday's or something or Applebee's, 'Two for $20,' you know what I mean?"[107]

Workers who are especially fatigued or pressed for time sometimes spring for a fast-food meal rather than cook. We asked one respondent, "…on top of [your SNAP] do you spend anything else on food?" She replied, "Yeah, because sometimes we run out or if I'm on the way to work or something and I haven't eaten then I'll have to stop and get something. But it's only like $10 probably a week because I'll go and get something off the $0.99 menu just to hold me."[108] Another said, "When I'm exhausted in the week and I just cannot look at the kitchen so it's like I'll buy [carry-out]."[109]

Losing SNAP benefits can also trigger fast-food meals, especially for those who cannot reserve enough cash from their regular income to undertake a major grocery-shopping trip or buy all the ingredients for a balanced meal. One respondent told us that the $1 menu at McDonald's was the cheapest way to provide a meal that had "all the different food groups." A McDonald's hamburger, she pointed out, contains bread, meat, cheese, and lettuce. Preparing a meal with that much variety at home, she said, would cost her much more.

---

[105] P81: Low Food Security, Other, Female, Age 29, 2-person household

[106] P73: Low Food Security, Black Non-Hispanic, Male, Age 38, 3-person household

[107] P65: Food Secure, Black Non-Hispanic, Male, Age 42, 3-person household

[108] P41: Very Low Food Security, Black Non-Hispanic, Female, Age 23, 2-person household

[109] P30: Very Low Food Security, Hispanic, Female, Age 29, 2-person household

C. Food Sharing Across Families and Households

Our respondents routinely share food with family members both within and outside their households. Typically, those with access to more resources or those with SNAP benefits help out family members who are struggling financially or lack SNAP benefits. In multigenerational households, it is typically the older members who provide for the younger. Usually, the families we interviewed are on the receiving end of food-sharing arrangements, but those who are on the giving end often find it challenging to provide the assistance they do offer, as we discussed in Chapter III.

When doubled up, Black Non-Hispanic households in our respondent group almost always share grocery and cooking duties across subfamilies, whereas subfamilies of other racial/ethnic groups are more likely to keep their food separate. When grocery shopping, most Black respondents whose families live with other families or individuals usually say they operate on the assumption that they are buying for everyone when they shop. Feeding the family is considered a joint effort, with the women putting their heads together to figure out how to feed everyone in the household. Even when Black subfamilies do buy just for themselves, it is often with the understanding that other subfamilies in the household may draw on these groceries if need be.

One Black mother lives in a household of 12, including her children, several of her siblings, her mother, and her grandmother. Together, they draw on a variety of resources to pay bills and buy food. At present, these include cash out of pocket, the respondent's SNAP benefits, her sister's disability check, and a small payout from a life insurance policy. Two members of the household, her mother and grandmother, have steady jobs, but the respondent and her sister do not; they braid hair or give plasma to close the gap when money for food is running short. She tells us,

> "We pull together. My grandma, she spends out of her pocket to get food and my mom will spend out of her pocket to go get food. Me, I spend out of my pocket [or use SNAP] to go get food and we'll be like "Oh, what are we going to eat today?" We'll come home with it and then if we completely don't have money, me and my sister will go give plasma so we have money to get food.
>
> (Interviewer: Okay, so is it like on a daily basis that you guys have these conversations?)
>
> Yeah.
>
> (Interviewer: Okay, so there isn't just one big grocery-shopping trip.)
>
> No, it's like every day we have to find something because we don't have…enough money [to buy everything at once]. We are paying bills [so] we just don't have enough money to just go grocery shopping because it's a lot of people that stay here [and the bills can run high]."[110]

Subfamilies in other racial/ethnic groups usually shop for groceries and cook separately. In a number of cases, individual families stored their food in their bedrooms. One multigenerational

---

[110] P48: Low Food Security, Black Non-Hispanic, Female, Age 19, 6-person household

household even had refrigerators in each bedroom for food storage.[111] But keeping food separate can be difficult when children are involved. We asked one Hispanic respondent, who was doubled up with her sisters, whether they shared food. She said, "I have my own groceries…, they have their own groceries. But sometimes my nephew, [it's] after school and he's just like, 'Can I get this?' or 'Can I get this?' And I can't say no, you know?"[112]

Sharing Food Outside the Household

Many respondents eat meals at the homes of relatives several times each week. However, our respondents almost never invite relatives or friends to their home for a meal. We asked one respondent, "Okay…, if people are stopping by, or relatives come over, that kind of gets tighter, not for you?" She replied, "That's not happening. We'll come to you but absolutely not! Are you kidding me?"[113]

Respondents may sometimes make an exception for their children's friends, who may stop by frequently, sometimes several at once. Teenage boys in particular can eat their way through a household's food reserve quickly. Many respondents face this situation with equanimity, because their children's friends are "just kids" and thus should not be denied. When these children come by, respondents try to provide food items that are cheap and that "stretch" such as garlic bread or potatoes. What follows is an example of a respondent who refuses to entertain her own friends in her home, but cannot say no to her children's friends.

> "I don't allow [my] friends to just drop in like that. If they do they bring their own provisions. I won't short my kids for other people.
>
> (Interviewer: What about your son's friends? Do they ever come by and…?)
>
> Oh they come by; they know enough to bring a sandwich (laughter, which makes it clear she is teasing). No, I'll pull a fish out of the freezer. My son's got two or three friends; I'll fry up some fish. That's one thing I can say, my kids' friends all love my cooking.
>
> (Interviewer: Does it put a strain on you though to have a few more mouths to feed?)
>
> It does but I'm old-fashioned; I cannot not do it. I can't have 5 pieces of fish when there are seven kids there. I just can't do it; it would break my heart to have to do that."[114]

Some, though, are less tolerant of the situation. A few are reduced to hiding food before their children's friends arrive, telling them point blank that they cannot afford to fix them a snack, or asking the parents of these children to pay for that food. One tells us,

---

[111] P61: Very Low Food Security, Other, Male, Age 22, 5-person household

[112] P28: Low Food Security, Hispanic, Female, Age 27, 3-person household

[113] P43: Low Food Security, Black Non-Hispanic, Female, Age 54, 2-person household

[114] P12: Very Low Food Security, Other, Male, Age 57, 3-person household

"Oh my God. I have kids, and kids bring friends and I feel so bad because sometimes I don't have it and I can't offer it. But it's just like, when it's there I can't just hide the food. I feel so embarrassed sometimes and I tell the kids - I try to tell them, the kids - "We don't have much food, you have to understand." But you know they're kids; they don't understand. They bring everyone over and it's like "Come on, let's eat.""

(Interviewer: So what do you do?)

Sometimes I have to give it up. And a lot of times I know [they are coming and] I hide it before they get there. And then I say, "Oh, your friends have to go, you have to come and eat," and then sit them down and they eat, and then I say, "Okay, you can go out now." But sometimes they catch me off guard, like get there before I put the food away. That's part of life."[115]

Another respondent relates the following story:

"Once my daughter had a friend stay a few days and yes, she consumed a lot of [food], so I had no other choice but to ask the lady not to bring the child anymore because it was getting out of hand. My daughter is not a big eater—she will consume a fruit or juice, but it's not in a large abundance like this little girl. [The girl] would ask me to cook, and I cooked and she asked for more servings. And then she would open the refrigerator and help herself without asking permission. I don't know if this child was fed at home….

She would come directly from school…. When her mom came to pick her up, I spoke to her and I told her that I didn't think that [the girl] ate so much. I told her that if [her daughter] asked for a juice, [the girl] asked for two; if I served some food she would ask for another serving. [I told her,] "I'm sorry, but you are going to have to give me some money so that I could replenish some of the items she consumed." I told her that I could barely make it to feed my daughter and was not able to feed more."[116]

Special Occasions

There is one other exception to the no-entertaining rule many respondents follow: most feel it imperative to invite the extended family over and provide cake, ice cream, and other treats for their children's birthday celebrations or graduations. Many purchase and prepare the food for these celebrations themselves, while others ask relatives to contribute to a potluck-style meal.

On holidays, however, families feel no such imperative, and only rarely host celebrations. A surprising number of respondents simply spend holidays by themselves, citing their inability to afford entertaining. Some attend charity dinners at churches and other community venues. But many attend large gatherings with extended family, especially for Thanksgiving and Christmas. In these

---

[115] P57: Low Food Security, Hispanic, Female, Age 42, 6-person household

[116] P31: Very Low Food Security, Hispanic, Female, Age 30, 2-person household

cases, respondents typically contribute one dish to the meal, often because their relatives understand their economic constraints. One explains, "Usually we all go to my aunt's house [for special occasions]. They know me they know my situation, so they just tell me to bring mashed potatoes and then there's the meal."[117]

When respondents do entertain, some rely on credit cards to fund the additional expenses. Most in this sample, however, use their SNAP and skimp on food for the rest of the month. One woman even saved a portion of her SNAP benefits for six months in order to celebrate her daughter's birthday in style:

> "Well for my daughter's birthday...I had to buy all the food because it's my daughter. But I knew [I had to begin to prepare in] January because my daughter's birthday's in July. So since January I kept saving out of my food stamps—$50, $50, $50, $50.... I mean, like I said, I just saved and like I said—budget, budget, budget.... I was going to have a cookout for my daughter so I knew this in January and decided [to start saving]. Because when you have no money, you gotta think months ahead and save for that one occasion, even if it's $20 a month."[118]

D. Health and Food

We asked each respondent to describe what "healthy eating" means to them, what their unhealthiest food habits are, what they would purchase that they do not purchase now if their funds were unlimited, and how they accommodate their children's food preferences. For most, healthy eating means fresh fruits and vegetables. Most named greasy or high-sugar foods as the unhealthiest components of their diet. Many said they would purchase healthier foods if they had more money to spend, but eating healthy simply costs more. Some households had children who were picky eaters. Such children consumed less nutritious food than households with children who ate whatever they were given.

Healthy Eating

Respondents generally claimed that at least at dinnertime, their families ate balanced meals. Many provided concrete examples of the balanced meals they planned and served at dinner. They were also quite forthcoming about unhealthy eating habits.

When asked what, in their view, constituted a healthy diet, respondents almost always cited fruits and vegetables as key. Several also noted the importance of drinking a lot of water (which typically meant bottled water). Most thought it was essential that all food groups be represented in one's diet, and at the dinner meal. Some mentioned the importance of "portion control."

In an effort to reduce consumption of fat, a few respondents bake their meats instead of frying them. One woman even talked at length about the importance of using "good oil" (e.g., olive oil). Opinions varied about juices and their nutritional value. Many felt that juices were full of sugar and

---

[117] P40: Very Low Food Security, White Non-Hispanic, Female, Age 33, 3-person household

[118] P83: Food Secure, Black Non-Hispanic, Female, Age 26, 2-person household

should be limited or avoided. Some respondents did include juice in their list of "healthy foods" and elected to buy juice instead of soda.

Many households defined healthy eating as consuming a protein, a starch, and a vegetable at dinner. We asked one respondent, "Do you wish that they had more healthy food or do you think they're pretty good on that?" She told us,

> "They're pretty good on that because that's what's on the plate. I mean, you're hungry and you're going to eat what's on the plate and what's on the plate is always a meat, some kind of rice or pasta, and a vegetable. Always. That's always on there.
>
> (Interviewer: Yeah, I noticed that when you were talking earlier; you had three slots you were filling with every meal.)
>
> Yeah. Always. Always, always, always."[119]

Unhealthiest Food Habits

Fried or greasy food, high-sugar foods (candy, cookies, and other dessert), chips and other snacks, and soda were identified as the least healthy foods in respondents' diets. Some respondents tied unhealthy eating habits to ethnic traditions. Hispanic respondents often noted that they were raised eating meals consisting of rice, beans and meat, and fried foods.[120] Many said it was a struggle to change those habits now by replacing starches with healthier foods like salads. One told us,

> "It's probably…cultural, you're used to certain things. We eat fried chicken, fried pork, no salad, plantains, everything deep fried. It's more of what you're used to, what you're accustomed to than anything else. So to try to tell me that salads…and fruits are much better for you than my fried chicken! It's like, it's hard. I mean, I know much more better now since I'm here, you know. So, it's hard to kind of break the routine. It is. Um, yeah.
>
> (Interviewer: No, I completely get that. I mean, my husband and I just love potatoes. And all we want to do is fry potatoes….)
>
> I mean, it's the same thing. Even with your kids. You try to not bring them up the way you were brought up but it's hard. She already doesn't eat certain vegetables and I try to eat more of them to show her to eat them."[121]

---

[119] P65: Food Secure, Black Non-Hispanic, Male, Age 42, 3-person household

[120] Only five respondents mentioned food practices unique to their culture/ethnicity. Cultural practices could affect either patterns of purchasing or types of foods consumed. For example, some Hispanic respondents in Texas mentioned that they purchased meat only at La Michoacana, a Mexican meat market chain. A Libyan respondent said she purchased meal from a Halal market, and a respondent of Indian origin shopped for groceries at an Indian market. Other respondents shopped at "ethnic" stores on occasion as well, but because of lower prices, not cultural practices.

[121] P17: Food Secure, Black Non-Hispanic, Female, Age 33, 2-person household

How Children's Tastes Shape Healthy and Unhealthy Eating

Many respondents claimed their children were picky eaters. We said to one, "...some parents tell us that they want their children to eat healthier but the children don't want to." She responded,

"That's why I want to [make my daughter eat healthy] now because she's little. Because later when she's older it will be the same as with me—now that I'm older I don't like to eat vegetables.

(Interviewer: And what was I going to say - and any time have you tried to give her something healthier and she has refused it?)

Yes.... She didn't eat it. She spits it out....

(Interviewer: What food was it?)

I tried giving her carrots because at WIC they told me to try and give the vegetables by hand. She does like broccoli a little bit, but [only] broccoli in Chinese food."[122]

However, a surprising number of respondents also said their children had large appetites and ate any dish that was put before them. We asked one respondent, "Are there any times that you try to do that and the kids just don't want it, they resist?"

"He eats everything. He'll eat all kinds of meats; he'll eat all the vegetables. He eats basically what's put on his plate. He'll pretty much finish his plate. He's not picky, oh I don't like green beans, no he'll eat it.... I haven't had a vegetable that he don't like.

(Interviewer: That's great. What about the baby?)

She eats it all too, she's not a fussy eater."[123]

Another shared a similar story,

"I started [feeding my children vegetables] way back, you know, like we're doing with my grandbaby, we start like he eats vegetables already. He doesn't have no problem with vegetables and stuff, and that's the key, you have to start young. You can't, you know, your kids get older now, you make a change and you expect, not going to happen."[124]

Some respondents noted that their children ate healthy food if an ingredient they liked (such as cheese) was added to a dish they would not otherwise eat (like vegetables or meats that are baked rather than fried). Several respondents boast that they "trick" their children into eating healthy food in this way. One explained,

---

[122] P72: Food Secure, Hispanic, Female, Age 21, 2-person household

[123] P82: Food Secure, White Non-Hispanic, Male, Age 31, 3-person household

[124] P25: Low Food Security, Black Non-Hispanic, Female, Age 43, 4-person household

"You hide the vegetables in the food. You get clever and creative.... You have to start early with that. So you buy the spaghetti sauce with the vegetables already in it. Now they have to eat their food.... It just became a habit.... I don't generally fry foods. It's very rare that I'll fry something. So they've always been accustomed to having it baked [as long as I disguise it with something they like]. They eat pretty healthy as far as that goes. They eat pretty good meals that are not a lot of fat in them.... You trick them. That's how you get them to eat healthy. You start young and you trick them."[125]

Though parents often want to instill healthy eating habits in their children, they also want to treat them. And the impulse to provide a "treat" may override nutritional concerns—similar to the dynamic with snacks. We asked one parent, "So what would you say are your healthiest habits in your family?"

"Healthiest habits? We don't drink soda. We—I drink a lot of water so I tend to make her drink water, too. Yep. She loves juice.... So I try to eat a little healthy..., but then I still want her to be a kid. So like every two weeks..., when I have the extra money, I'll treat her. [This] time of year we'll go for ice cream a lot more and then I always—every other Friday, we'll go to McDonald's or Burger King or something...so she don't feel like she's not like other kids. [But] I try not to, you know."[126]

The Ideal Grocery List: Respondent Opinions

When respondents were asked what foods they would buy if they had an unlimited amount of money, many claimed that they would purchase healthier food. We said to one respondent, "People have a lot of different ideas about what healthy eating means for them; tell me about what you think of that."

"I have a brother that is [an athlete in] training so he is always preaching to us. 'Stay away from the sugar! Stay away the starch! Eat a lot of fruit! Eat a lot of vegetables! Stay away from pork, it's not good. Stay away from the beef, it's not good.' But we still eat it because we can't just afford all fish and chicken—all of the healthy stuff—on SNAP. You can't afford it all. If I could eat healthy I would love to eat healthy because I love fruit and vegetables."[127]

Like this respondent, most said they would like to buy healthier foods—particularly fruit, vegetables, leaner meats, and fish–but could not afford to. A number specifically noted a desire to purchase organic food that had not been treated with chemicals. Only one was able to do so consistently, because her children's father, who lived with the family, was a manager at Whole Foods and received a discount. Another respondent, who could not purchase organic products with any regularity, told us that if she had an unlimited food budget,

---

[125] P7: Very Low Food Security, White Non-Hispanic, Female, Age 41, 4-person household

[126] P81: Low Food Security, Other, Female, Age 29, 2-person household

[127] P16: Low Food Security, Black Non-Hispanic, Female, Age 37, 3-person household

"I definitely would buy more organic stuff. That would make a big difference. Since I got hit with this sickness, [buying organic has made] a big difference. But it's really expensive buying organic stuff. It's expensive. If it's on sale I buy it, but it's hardly on sale…. So yeah, if I had an unlimited amount of money, I would definitely choose organic stuff and just some of the stuff that you want to buy but it's expensive; instead of the rice I would want to buy whole grain rice or something, but it's more expensive than the white rice."[128]

A few respondents said their food-purchasing habits would not change in any way with an influx of additional funds, while some others noted that they would merely purchase more of everything they already bought. Several fantasized about eating out more frequently, or indulging in lobster or steak. Many said they would like to provide their children with more of the treats they often begged for in the grocery store (sometimes fruit, but often items like frozen mini-pizzas or ice cream).

E. Chapter V Summary

Respondents generally ate light breakfasts, simple lunches, and what they perceive as balanced dinners; these patterns are less consistent with lower food security families, who often eat starchy meals or are more likely to regularly skip meals entirely. Most made an effort to allow for the purchase of small luxuries for their children, afternoon snacks, like an ice cream or meal at McDonald's every few weeks. Many families avoid sharing food even when doubled up. Families almost never entertained, even on holidays, because they could not afford it. The exception was children's birthday parties or graduations; some parents planned ahead for months to be able to afford the food this small celebration entailed. SNAP participants admit that their habits are not as healthy as they could be, but cite the greater expense of more nutritious or healthy foods as the cause.

At the same time, parents do try to adjust their children's diets to include vegetables, and avoid fried foods. They also strive to ensure that dinner is a balanced meal representing all the food groups. Many claimed that their families had learned to eat healthy with the foods they could afford; for example, a few baked their meats instead of frying them, many bought frozen vegetables so that they could provide them at every meal, and some emphasized drinking lots of water. Certain health issues were prevalent among our respondents at all levels of food security, including anxiety, diabetes, and food allergies. Because of the limited choices their food budgets permit, many families find it difficult to accommodate the various health needs of their members.

---

[128] P57: Low Food Security, Hispanic, Female, Age 42, 6-person household

This page has been left blank for double-sided copying.

VI. WHAT IS THE ROLE OF SNAP IN HELPING HOUSEHOLDS MEET FAMILY FOOD NEEDS?

What are respondents' experiences when they apply for SNAP benefits, how long do they stay in the program, and what do they like best and least about SNAP? Most applied in the face of an economic shock; usually job loss, loss of a partner, a pregnancy, childbirth, or health issue that limited work. Most respondents reported that SNAP helped them significantly to weather the financial shocks, and several referred to SNAP as a "lifesaver." Some said that SNAP also allowed them to purchase foods of better quality or more variety than they otherwise could have. Respondents had a multitude of complaints about SNAP, however. Many complained that their benefits did not last the whole month. Though SNAP was never designed to provide all of families' food needs for all households (see Chapter IV), it is a common perception that the benefits ought to do so. Perhaps due to this expectation, many families fail to set aside cash for food, and instead earmark their cash for other bills. This is not surprising, since these households are often living in the red.

Families also expressed frustration over their treatment by caseworkers, the overwhelming paperwork demands, the inflexibility of the process, the opacity and, in their view, unfairness of eligibility determinations, and the amount of time they had to spend waiting in line, often repeatedly, at their local SNAP office to apply for and maintain their SNAP benefits. Another primary complaint about SNAP was interruption, reduction, or loss of benefits without warning. Respondents seldom received any nutritional information or guidance from SNAP, but SNAP beneficiaries who were also WIC participants often said the WIC program was a valuable source of nutritional information. Respondents shared a number of ideas of how SNAP might be improved.

A. SNAP Participation Patterns

Enrolling in SNAP

Past quantitative research has suggested that changes in household structure or economic circumstances frequently precede entry into assistance programs (Mabli et al. 2011). Consistent with this, most IDI respondents applied for SNAP as a result of an abrupt change in income or household size or composition. For some, this event was childbirth, a loss of income due to a job loss, loss of income due to reduced hours, or the loss of a wage-earning partner due to death, divorce or breakup, or incarceration. Natural disasters can also lead to a spike in SNAP applications. A few of our respondents in Texas said they sought food assistance after Hurricane Ike, which had not only affected food availability and prices, they claimed, but also caused them to lose their jobs or have their work hours reduced.

Length of SNAP Tenure

Our respondents have been receiving SNAP benefits for varied lengths of time, from a few weeks to several years. Few have been continuously on SNAP; most report that changes in income and household size have rendered them ineligible from time to time, and they have had to reapply when times got tougher again. For example, we asked one respondent, "Tell me, when did you first apply for SNAP"?

"I first applied when Destiny was very young and at the time I didn't qualify. Then I applied again and I only qualified for $16 because I was making quite a bit of money. Then…when I lost my job, I think I waited about a year and I applied again. We got it and I think I had had it for about three months and then you know she [went to live with her dad] so I reported that she wasn't with me so again, I didn't qualify for food stamps. So in July of last year, she came back. I waited, and I applied in February…and I qualified."[129]

B. What Respondents Like Most About SNAP

Several respondents referred to SNAP as a "lifesaver," a testament to the extent to which SNAP benefits affect the lives of the families we interviewed. Almost all respondents said that what they liked most about the program is that it eased their monthly budget struggle—they could devote more of their cash to their bills—and it helped them place more and higher-quality food on their tables because it provided resources that could only be devoted to food and could not be traded off in the face of other financial demands. With SNAP benefits to draw on, families felt less pressed to juggle bills and other payments to make room in the monthly budget for food. We asked one respondent, "What do you like the most about SNAP?" She replied, "They help me and how much we save because that's money that we're saving towards either a bill or anything extra. With little kids, diapers and stuff like that."[130] In addition, many reported an alleviation of anxiety and stress; figuring out how to feed the family when cash resources had run dry ceased to be an often epic struggle.

We asked one respondent who had had two recent spells of unemployment, the first without any SNAP, "So let's think back to the time that you didn't have SNAP, and your unemployment spell, how was that different than this time around?"

"I'm much better off financially [after my job this time], because [then] I had no [SNAP]. The last time it was extreme struggle, because I had no idea. I mean food was killing me….

(Interviewer: So tell me more about that time. So were you able to make bills in the same way that you're…)

It was hard. I was behind. Yes, I was seriously behind…. I was having to call and make payment plans on all of my bills. And I was [seeking] deferred payment, "Can I pay half this?" because it was a struggle—it was. Yes….

(Interviewer: Anything else that you had to do in that time to get through?)

No…. Thank God, I [became] employed. Someone hired me."[131]

---

[129] P66: Low Food Security, Hispanic, Female, Age 64, 2-person household

[130] P20: Low Food Security, Hispanic, Female, Age 23, 4-person household

[131] P43: Low Food Security, Black Non-Hispanic, Female, Age 54, 2-person household

We asked another, "So you applied six months back. Okay. What do you like best about SNAP?"

> "Well I just like the freedom of buying what I can for my son and not like having to worry about, 'Oh, I can't afford to buy this because even though it's better quality, I can't afford it so we have to go with the cheap stuff that's maybe not so good for you or whatever,' so I just like that I have that liberty to be able to [buy the healthier stuff]."[132]

C. What Respondents Like Least About SNAP

Too Much Red Tape/Overly Rigid Process

Many respondents complained that the process of applying for SNAP benefits was long and complex. Some also claimed that the treatment they received when applying was demeaning. For any given SNAP office, there is often a reasonably strict sequence for the filing of paperwork, in-person appointments, mailings, and phone calls. Respondents claim that even small departures from this sequence—even missing a phone call—can result in a benefit termination or a delay in receiving SNAP benefits. In sum, the system is perceived as overly rigid—many claim that the smallest technicality can result in benefit terminations or delay.

One respondent related the following story:

> "Like when I applied for Food Stamps, it took literally four months to get approved because even though I took all the information down there in their office, left it in their box, that lady claimed she didn't get it and then she sent me a letter that I did not get and so it was like a back and forth thing and then they cancelled my application and I had to start all over again....

> It was bad.... It was crazy. I bought all kinds of stuff. I bought so much food; I ate and ate and ate. That was the only time I did that was the first time I got Food Stamps because I was hungry. You know..., I needed help but no..., they're not interested in helping you. They're interested in just doing the absolute minimum that they have to do in order to get you out of their office."[133]

We said to another respondent, "Tell me about your interaction with the office or what you think about the processes."

> "The process? It takes a while.... They tell you we have within 30 days but a lot of times, the caseworkers...., they'll take longer than 30 days.

> (Interviewer: ...How often do you have to update your file?)

---

[132] P30: Very Low Food Security, Hispanic, Female, Age 29, 2-person household

[133] P7: Very Low Food Security, White Non-Hispanic, Female, Age 41, 4-person household

You're supposed to do it like every six months reoccurring but there have a been a few times like it lapsed and I send the paper back right away and I was like a day or [so late]. If you're even one day off, they cut you off completely. There's no like consideration, no nothing.

(Interviewer: And then what happens?)

You struggle.

(Interviewer: When will they consider you again?)

Not until—like they have 30 days to process it…. It takes like a whole month.

(Interviewer: So that'll be one month that you don't get any SNAP at all?)

Yeah and then because you applied for that month, sometimes [you'll] get the amount [you were missing] back, [but that] doesn't help you for the month that you didn't have it. Yeah, I [may] have a lot of money this month but it doesn't help me for last month when I didn't have it."[134]

Many feel that performing all the necessary checks to ensure eligibility is warranted the first time around, but having these steps/questions/verifications repeated each time they are recertified or have to reapply for benefits is time-consuming and viewed as unnecessary. According to some, the practices are even insulting. In the words of one respondent,

"Well, what I like most about it, of course, is the help. That's one less bill or one less expense that I need worry about. And what I like least about it is…they gave it to me for a couple of months, then they said I didn't qualify again. [They said my husband[had made too much money. So they cut me off and I was off for like two months or something. Two or three months. And then I told them his hours had gone down, so I took in the new pay stubs to show them what he was making. And they said I had to essentially reapply. I said, 'Well, why is [my case] still open? Why do I get the letters?' They're like, 'Well, it's essentially just like reapplying.'

So I was like, okay. So I had to make an appointment, go in, go through all this stuff again. Bring in all this paperwork. And then I got it again for—this will be the third month. And [they just sent me a letter that] it was time for a recertification again. I was like, "I just did it. And you guys said—the paper that I got said it was good for a year!" And they're like, "Well, you still need to come in." So, I was like, "Okay". So I went in and took in the new stubs. And he probably got five hours more [last month] than he got last time [we applied], and now we don't qualify. It's frustrating."[135]

---

[134] P50: Low Food Security, Hispanic, Female, Age 22, 3-person household

[135] P2: Low Food Security, Hispanic, Female, Age 45, 3-person household

Interruption in SNAP Benefits Without Warning

In addition to frustrations with the red tape associated with accessing SNAP benefits, another common complaint was that SNAP benefits had been interrupted, reduced, or cancelled without warning. Program regulations call for providing participants with information about key anticipated case actions. However, either these case action notifications were not always sent to (or received by) respondents, or else the respondents may not have understood them. In any event, multiple respondents shared stories of having their benefits reduced without prior notification. When the changes in benefits occurred, this caused severe financial strain; in this small sample, benefit loss was a common trigger of food hardship among those the survey found to be food insecure, as we show in Chapter VI. Although sometimes these changes were made in error and were eventually fixed, most changes were for reasons that respondents did not understand, which we discuss next.

Disagree With or Do Not Understand Rules

Many respondents were frustrated about what they felt were unjustified cuts to their SNAP benefits. Most did not understand why their SNAP amount had been reduced or why they were no longer eligible for SNAP, and claimed changes were unwarranted because their household and financial circumstances had not changed, or had not changed very much. Others were outraged that necessities like cars were considered luxuries and counted against them when their benefits were tallied.[136] For example,

> "They count the fact that I have a car…. I have to have because of doctors and stuff like that…. I have a machine under my bed that monitors my heart. And I have to have a car if an emergency happens. They look at that as a luxury but in my mind it's a necessity. It's a lot. It's a lot. I won't do it no more. I won't go back there no more.
>
> (Interviewer: And they didn't understand when you were like 'No, this is not a luxury. This is a medical necessity.')
>
> They didn't care. It took a lot for me to go there. Oh my God, it took a lot.
>
> (Interviewer: How was that?)
>
> Actually, I went off on them. I went off because I felt like it shouldn't matter what's on the paper [about the car]. I'm not just a guy who wants to come in and try to beat the system. I needed the help all the time. They wasn't trying to hear it so I cussed them out. To me it's just not fair sometimes…. I'm not going to take from the system if I don't really need it."[137]

We asked another, "Okay. What do you like best about Food Stamps?"

---

[136] Technically, the existence of one or more vehicles does not affect the benefit level. However, it can, under some circumstances, affect eligibility.

[137] P73: Low Food Security, Black Non-Hispanic, Male, Age 38, 3-person household

"That you don't have to buy [food] out of cash and you can use the Food Stamps. That's what kind of I like is kind of handy but [what] I hate [is] how they often cut your Food Stamps knowing, [even] if you get the same income, they'll still cut it and that's what I don't like.... That happened a couple of months to me. They had lowered it down to $200 something. I was getting $200 something and they lowered it down a little more and I was kind of mad and I wanted to call them with like why [when] I was still getting the same income.

[Then] I was cut off one month. That was—I want to say March. I was cut off because they claim that I didn't show up for my interview and stuff and I didn't know [I was supposed to] show up. They tell me they sent something to my address. And then I went up there and I was cut off for that—they said because [I had not reported a change of] address. I said [I] used to get my mail [forwarded]. Why is it not getting [forwarded] now [all of a sudden]? So I got cut off and I didn't end up getting...my Food Stamps [until] like real late."[138]

Long Wait Times at SNAP Office

Many also complained about the length of the wait times at their local SNAP offices. One respondent told us about the frustrating process of setting up and waiting for an appointment at his local office,

"A lady I know applied online. People had told me that they would come in and wait for about six hours [so I wanted to avoid that]. She said that I could go online and they would give me an appointment. Well I got the appointment. Well I had to work so I had to reschedule my appointment.

So they rescheduled it for three days later. People were passing out in the office because it was overcrowded in there. It was also really hot that day. I was standing in line for three hours. Once I was seen I had to wait another two hours to see someone else. I was actually there from 8:00 to 4:45. The supervisor came out and took me into her office. Then they said because you do work, we'll have to mail the card to you. Usually they give the cards out while you are there. But that is only for the people that do not have jobs.

I didn't receive my card so I had to go back up to the office and told them that I never received my card and the lady made me show ID and she gave me my LINK card right then. I really didn't know why they didn't do this the first time. I did get $280.00 on my card which was really nice."[139]

One respondent noted that the long wait times at the SNAP office had a direct negative impact on his wages.

---

[138] P59: Low Food Security, Black Non-Hispanic, Female, Age 22, 3-person household

[139] P62: Very Low Food Security, Black Non-Hispanic, Male, Age 36, 2-person household

"Your [lost hours are] deducted [from your pay] each time you leave work to go over there and to ask for help. You lose an hour of work and that's an hour that the company's not going to pay anyone. I went to talk to them to ask what's going on…. It's a two…hour wait each time. It's…always full of people looking for help and you have to get in line and wait and wait and wait…. And each time that I would go I would lose two hours of work or at least a two hours and a half, understand, and you don't get those back so your paycheck is lower."[140]

SNAP Caseworkers Are Rude

Poor treatment at their local SNAP offices is a common complaint. Respondents were asked, "What do you like least about the SNAP program?" The following response is typical:

"When you go to the offices…the people are rude. Not all of them, but it's when you go to the offices and the people, they talk to you in a [certain] way. When I first got Food Stamps, the one lady she talked to me like I was just 10. Then the next time I went in there I had to lay the line, "My kid don't even talk to me like this so we're not going to talk to each other like this." Sometimes they're just too rude. I don't know if it's because we're the ones that need help [or what]. Especially the one over there on [Name of Office], they're rude and the one down here is real rude."[141]

This treatment compounded many respondents' sense of shame about not being able to get by without government assistance. One respondent offered the following account:

"The thing that I like the least about it is that they want to pry into everything about your life and make it so difficult for you…. I don't care how much people evolve and how open minded they are, it's never going to be like you're royalty because you're on Food Stamps or on welfare. I mean seriously I've never seen anybody in my entire life ever run through the grocery store or up and down the streets going "Oh, we're on welfare. We're wonderful thank God! Yay!" or going through school going "We're on welfare and you're not"—like it's something so cool. It's degrading. It's embarrassing. It's shameful….

There have even been people that I know that they said they would rather starve to death than go through the embarrassment…of everything because it's like they want blood. They literally, almost literally want you to bleed for them in order to prove that you are poverty stricken enough that you need this. It's just completely ridiculous. It's like okay, I'm not going to come to you and tell you that I want you to give me Food Stamps or money or medical stuff if I don't really need it. I have these kids. They need to be taken care of and that's the only reason I go to Food Stamps. Because if it was me by myself I would starve half to death nearly every day and

---

[140] P74: Low Food Security, Hispanic, Male, Age 57, 5-person household

[141] P48: Low Food Security, Black Non-Hispanic, Female, Age 19, 6-person household

night [rather than go to Food Stamps for help]. But I have children, they are my only reason that I have food stamps that I go, that I apply, that I try to keep it."[142]

The quote below summarizes the general attitude respondents have toward the SNAP program: "So what has been your experience with the program…?" we asked.

"It is good; I have had some bad times. Most of the time it has done what I needed it to do and it is there for me. It is a pain […] to be honest. Some people are just hard to deal with and a lot of times you go to the office and it [is] hard. Sometimes I feel like [it might be because] there are a lot of people out there taking advantage of the system. [When I've been there] there are people that are clearly on their phones making drug calls and it just sucks. It makes it harder for the people that are actually there and need it. For instance, why do I have to show you my birth certificate? I was born here! What are you talking about? You are not going to give me this because you won't accept a copy? It is just a lot of paper work and being on time with your deadline and meeting the requirements that they have set for you."[143]

D. What Happens When There Is No SNAP in the Household?

Only 11 respondents reported that their SNAP benefits covered all their monthly household food expenses. As noted above, SNAP was not designed to meet this goal. Respondents used a variety of strategies (sometimes in combination) to acquire food once their SNAP benefits had been exhausted for the month. Many purchase some additional food with cash, though cash is hard to come by toward the end of the month, and families seldom reserve any of their cash resources for food in anticipation of the SNAP shortfall. Others rely on support from family members, garner food from churches or food pantries, or cut back on meeting other financial obligations in order to have sufficient cash for food. Others reduce the amount and/or types of food they purchase and consume. We cover these later themes under the "Coping Strategies" heading in Chapter III.

We said to one respondent, "…lots of people are struggling in trying to make ends meet in order to make it through to the end of the month. How has it been for your family?"

"Since I've been receiving the food stamps it's been a little better. I am able to buy the food for 15 days; sometimes we're able to make it to 22 days with the food stamps that I get; then we make more groceries for the last week.

(Interviewer: What do you do in order to purchase your food when your [Food Stamps] run out?)

I use cash, [basically].

(Interviewer: Out of your pocket?)

---

[142] P4: Very Low Food Security, White Non-Hispanic, Female, Age 35, 6-person household

[143] P3: Food Secure, White Non-Hispanic, Female, Age 28, 3-person household

Yes, out of pocket."[144]

We asked another, "...tell me about the last time that you lacked the money you needed for food."

> "Well how do I tell you? The problem as I explained to you, last month they gave me all of SNAP completely the month of April and this month they gave me only a portion. For example what is the date? Is it the 15th?

> (Interviewer: The 15th.)

> The 15th and everything is gone. It's all gone now from here to the end [of the month]. I am now taking it out of my pocket from the little bit that is left from my pay. And on top of that I need to keep aside a weekly amount for the rent and for the rest of the expenses that I explained to you, the gas, the electricity, the cable, and that's is what is happening because all the Food Stamps are all gone now. We make one big purchase and you know that with three children eating and everything is getting used…. That's how it is."[145]

E. SNAP/WIC and Nutrition Education

Almost all respondents said that SNAP does not provide any nutrition information, but WIC does. Respondents appreciated the nutritional information that WIC provides and said they felt their visits to the welfare office to procure SNAP were focused mostly on paperwork, eligibility, and benefit determination. This is not surprising, as SNAP caseworkers are not required to provide nutritional education. Other sources of nutrition information were scarce, but some named their doctor's office and their own internet/television research. One frustration respondents shared is that despite the nutrition information WIC and other venues provide, "healthy" food, such as fresh fruit and vegetables, is simply too expensive or too likely to "go bad" before it can be used. Therefore, they cannot always follow through on the advice they receive.

The SNAP Office—No Information, All Business

Almost across the board, respondents said that SNAP did not provide them with nutrition information. In the majority of cases, when asked if SNAP gave them information about nutrition, respondents answered by simply saying "no," or "nothing at all." Some noted they wouldn't know— they have not even been to the SNAP office because they applied online. Respondents sometimes volunteered the view that the SNAP program does not care about them as people or about their nutrition, and is concerned only about making sure they qualify and do not use SNAP for products that are not allowed. We asked one respondent, "What do they tell you at the SNAP office about what foods to eat and so on?"

> "No way. They don't care.

---

[144] P31: Very Low Food Security, Hispanic, Female, Age 30, 2-person household

[145] P74: Low Food Security, Hispanic, Male, Age 57, 5-person household

(Interviewer: Do they provide any information about nutritious foods or...?)

Absolutely not. I mean, they might have information down there but they don't present it to - their main focus is to get you processed through the program and verify the information you're giving them. They're not interested in how you spend money. I've never had that experience where somebody actually sat down and said, "We offer a food preparation program to teach you how to cook [healthy foods]." I pretty much had to teach myself or learn on TV and the internet. No one ever sat down and said, "Oh, you can save money - a lot of money if you do it this way...." The Food Stamp office could be very influential, I think, if they had other information or required that participants in the program take a class on how to prepare food and how to, or if they offered coupons preloaded [on the SNAP card to] encourage people...make the dollar go further."[146]

Many respondents said exactly the same thing: that when they went to the SNAP office, it was just "here is your card." In the words of one respondent: "At WIC they tell you to eat a lot of fresh vegetables, fruits and stuff like that. But at the food stamp office I don't remember it was pretty much just, 'Here is your card.'"[147]

WIC—Very Helpful

In contrast to SNAP, almost everyone who was on WIC said WIC does provide nutrition education; indeed, it is a required part of the program. Most respondents appreciated the information they received. Some had met with a dietician/nutritionist there, while others had their children weighed and lead levels tested. Others were required to watch nutrition/cooking videos, and some were able to practice cooking healthy meals. We asked one respondent, "And what about at the WIC office?"

"Really, really helpful and they care. Like every time you go, they will check the baby's weight. I really appreciate WIC. It's a really good program.

(Interviewer: They weigh him each time you go?)

Yeah, they have a check [up] time. It was three months, I guess. You don't have to reapply, so they make sure that everything is right and documents and all that. They care about your child's health and the lead, everything. They help in every way you imagine, like when I was breastfeeding, they gave me a pump and they gave me the electric pump."[148]

The theme that WIC is helpful in contrast to SNAP dominated the answers to our questions in this domain:

---

[146] P7: Very Low Food Security, White Non-Hispanic, Female, Age 41, 4-person household

[147] P36: Food Secure, White Non-Hispanic, Female, Age 19, 3-person household

[148] P11: Food Secure, White Non-Hispanic, Female, Age 32, 5-person household

"Yeah, WIC they're like a lot more into it. They give me like brochures about the steps, the triangle and all that stuff.

(Interviewer: The food pyramid?)

Yeah, the food pyramid. And they tell me, they asked me questions about my kids, what they drink, what they eat, how much juice or they give me tips about vegetables, making it fun and stuff. I think it's better at WIC because SNAP never told me that."[149]

Other Nutrition Information

A few respondents mentioned other sources of information, such as the doctor's office, a child protection worker from the Illinois Department of Children and Family Services, the internet or television, a drug rehabilitation program, and a child's school. One said, "The outpatient rehab that I'm going to, they helped with that a lot because we're, well we do parenting class. When I was in inpatient rehab we covered that a lot for our children."[150] Another told us, "The pediatrician yes, I love her. She's Hindu and she has a lot of beliefs, like old school beliefs. And she's like, 'No more bottle, he's two.' My Department of Children and Family Services social worker for the child [also] tells me no more bottle."[151] A third told us, "The doctors always tell us about, to stay away from certain stuff, especially…. Because the three of us, we're all, you know, big people."[152]

One respondent credited the dietician at a drug rehabilitation center where she received treatment for substance abuse.

"(Interviewer: …You said that you have a dietician [at the rehab center] and they tell you to eat little meals frequently. What else do they tell you about?)

Tell me what to stay away from, like I can't have sodas, the salt so I drink Crystal Lite, which my family has all got to change over to Crystal Lite. They just tell you basically what to stay away from, how much portions to eat, how much vegetables to have and stuff like that."[153]

Several said their main source of information was television or internet. We asked one, "So you mentioned Dr. Oz and Rachel Ray. Where do you get your information about healthy eating?"

"From them. And then I read a lot. I listen to other people's issues and kind of try to fix my issues. [On Dr. Oz], you got people coming to the hospital will tell you what they do, how they get to this age, how many cigarettes they smoke, how many they

---

[149] P20: Low Food Security, Hispanic, Female, Age 23, 4-person household

[150] P27: Low Food Security, Hispanic, Female, Age 31, 5-person household

[151] P27: Low Food Security, Hispanic, Female, Age 31, 5-person household

[152] P8: Very Low Food Security, Hispanic, Female, Age 32, 3-person household

[153] P73: Low Food Security, Black Non-Hispanic, Male, Age 38, 3-person household

drank. So I look at my life and I say, 'Ah, I can better that if I do this.' You know? You know, [and] I watch The Biggest Loser."[154]

Another told us,

"Well I do a lot of my own like online [research] and stuff. They have a lot of the healthy—the websites about health and feeding your children and stuff like that so I look them up at those kinds of pages and just get ideas on like vegetables and stuff and different ways to introduce them to him."[155]

F. Other Food Programs

WIC was the only food program other than SNAP that our respondents participated in with any frequency. Respondents had varying thoughts about WIC. As has been indicated previously, for the most part, people were very positive about it. Several offered powerful testimonials about how WIC is what got them through the month, and some talked about how they had enough food until they lost WIC, and then no longer had enough. A few people had to discontinue WIC because they were unable to make it to appointments. Some stopped participating because they did not like that WIC weighed their children and gave them nutrition advice. For the most part, however, respondents were positive about WIC, and for many respondents it was a major reason they avoided food hardship.

We asked one respondent, "So what do you like best about WIC?" She replied, "What do I like best? It gets you through the month."[156] Another answered that question as follows: "That I get like the milk and the eggs and the cheese, like all the little things that I get, that's saving me from wasting on my food stamps. So that's one little good benefit I have for it. And I get it until she's five, so that's good."[157]

Several respondents talked about how WIC had made the difference in allowing them to have enough food each month, and how once their children aged out, things got tougher. One said,

"You know what I wish is that I still could get WIC. Do you know that WIC program?

(Interviewer: Yeah.)

Cheese, cereal and milk. That would save me so much money, but she's too old for that. But yeah, that's what I put back [at the grocery store] the most, is cheese because right when I get to the end, I realize oh, $4.00, $3.00, you know?"[158]

---

[154] P81: Low Food Security, Other, Female, Age 29, 2-person household

[155] P30: Very Low Food Security, Hispanic, Female, Age 29, 2-person household

[156] P28: Low Food Security, Hispanic, Female, Age 27, 3-person household

[157] P49: Food Secure, Hispanic, Female, Age 24, 6-person household

[158] P10: Low Food Security, Hispanic, Female, Age 37, 2-person household

Another shared a similar story, "When I was actually getting WIC for both of my kids, it was enough. It was more than enough, actually. I didn't have to complain; I always had enough food for them. But now that I'm only getting WIC for one, it's harder."[159]

Most respondents first learned of WIC through their doctor, usually when they were pregnant. A few said a SNAP caseworker referred them to WIC, and some said that family members told them about the program.

Many liked the fact that WIC limited the type of food a family could acquire, because it virtually guaranteed healthy eating. One respondent said,

> "I think it's a good program because they only allow you to get milk, juice, cheese, and the healthy cereal that's how I started eating the Honey Oats and all that. Beans. I think that they give you peanut butter. So I think that it's really good. And now they give you like a $10 in your WIC card for fruits and vegetables only. So that's good."[160]

Additionally, respondents also say the WIC offices themselves, and the treatment they receive there, is also very positive, especially in contrast to the SNAP offices. One respondent compared the WIC and SNAP offices, saying,

> "The WIC office was actually very pleasant. Sometimes you go to the Food Stamp office, you know, you have to sit in there and there's all these people and kids popping up. But, no, [WIC] just kind of send[s] you in and nowadays it's, like, it's really nice. You just do things on the internet. You take all the tests with them, and they upload the card and you're good, you know?"[161]

Another contrasted WIC and SNAP in this way, "WIC has been pretty good because WIC is fast. Like they—whoever handles WIC, they just see you right there. They're always very fast, like out of there. You don't have to wait like no time. They're very on top of everything. The people are courteous…." Another explained that "Paperwork for WIC is also more—it's simpler than that for Food Stamps."[162]

Even though the majority of respondents were positive about WIC, some did say that the frequent appointments and check-ins required were difficult to attend and in some cases, were not helpful. Some respondents stopped participating in the program because of this. We asked one mother, "Have you ever been on WIC before?" She explained, "I signed up on it out here but I had trouble, like I just got a car to where I can go back and forth places it before [I had it] I had problems getting to my appointments and stuff. So I missed the appointment for the WIC."[163]

---

[159] P58: Very Low Food Security, Hispanic, Female, Age 28, 3-person household

[160] P34: Very Low Food Security, Hispanic, Female, Age 28, 5-person household

[161] P77: Very Low Food Security, White Non-Hispanic, Female, Age 25, 2-person household

[162] P28: Low Food Security, Hispanic, Female, Age 27, 3-person household

[163] P14: Food Secure, White Non-Hispanic, Female, Age 30, 3-person household

G. Respondents' Ideas About How SNAP Could Be More Supportive

When respondents talked about food and SNAP, several themes came up repeatedly. First, many respondents talked about food becoming just too expensive, and they wish the government could do more to regulate food prices. Second, many respondents thought they needed more help from SNAP, and said they wish SNAP took expenses, and not just income, into account. Respondents also talked about the need for more information about nutrition and how to budget. Respondents did not talk about these latter needs for themselves, but rather noted they felt others needed such education.

Food is Too Expensive

Many respondents talked about how expensive food is, and how they felt the amount of money they receive from SNAP has not kept up with other price increases. In fact, under program rules, benefits levels are set to reflect food price changes. Nevertheless, it is useful to identify respondent perceptions on this issue.

One respondent shared this view: "Well the cost of living has gone up so I think the cost of living in Food Stamps should rise also. It should be budgeted on expense."[164] Another said,

> "…the little bit of money that I get really doesn't help. I mean, it helps but it really doesn't help because the food cost, the food is so high. The cost of everything is so high so they've got to take that into consideration a little bit more. They can't raise the price of steak or chicken and expect you to still get the same amount. Our cost of living jumps up a dollar when something else jumps up $3.00. Remember back in the day $120 would have been a lot. Now it actually doesn't mean nothing. It's just a little more reconsideration as far as the average person goes."[165]

Another also commented on the rising cost of food, and the failure of SNAP to help families adjust to these increases,

> "These grocery companies should have a ceiling put on their products so that they couldn't be gouging people like they are. There's no reason for a person to have to pay $2-$3 for one stupid beefsteak tomato when one plant grows 50 of them, especially when they're doing it in July. That's what's going on; too much corporate greed. All of the small mom and pop stores are gone and the big ones don't [care] about anything when they've got more than they can ever use in a lifetime themselves."[166]

Several noted that given their expenses, "just a little bit more" would help. One told us, "The only thing that I could say is that it would be nice if they could give me little bit more to work it out. But they're not, SNAP is not really adding up the things that we pay, you know. They're just adding

---

[164] P31: Very Low Food Security, Hispanic, Female, Age 30, 2-person household

[165] P73: Low Food Security, Black Non-Hispanic, Male, Age 38, 3-person household

[166] P12: Very Low Food Security, Other, Male, Age 57, 3-person household

up what we make. It's hard."[167] Another said, "Maybe if they keep it a little bit more on the food stamps. A little bit more on the Food Stamps and yeah... $70, $80 more, just a little bit more."[168]

Administrative/Program Improvements

Suggested administrative improvements were the flip side of many of the complaints about SNAP. These suggestions include having a shorter interval between filing for SNAP and receiving benefits, advance notice of any changes in benefits, clearer explanation of the rules associated with benefits, and less red tape.

One respondent shared the opinion that,

"...the program should be designed a little better.

(Interviewer: Your thoughts on that?)

Just in general, the way that they work. I mean, they have no concern for anybody. Like if you go past one day, I think I was like - I had it by 1:00 and I sent it at 3:00 and they denied it and I had to wait 30 more days.

(Interviewer: More flexibility?)

More flexibility in the program and just faster, I guess, because the 30 days [is a long time]. [And] sometimes whenever you talk to the caseworker, they're really rude. They don't care."[169]

Several respondents suggested having some kind of play area in the SNAP office so children could be entertained during the long wait times.

Finally, several talked about the need for classes about budgeting and nutrition. Interestingly, not a single respondent who raised this issue wanted such classes for themselves; instead, they all talked about seeing other SNAP recipients either wasting money due to a lack of budgeting/efficient food buying and/or buying unhealthy food.

"Give them classes on nutrition - nutritional classes - because a lot of time people buy food but it's not really healthy food. And in the end, you run through it so fast it doesn't even matter if you have food or not because the calories that you are eating, they've done burned off as soon as you've ate them because it's bad food. So I think they should have nutritional classes. And if, they should have weigh-ins to make sure that you're monitoring these families because I see a lot of people that have, I know, I know the food - you know, people say you know who get Food Stamps because they have three or four baskets of stuff. But I think you should help them with that.

---

[167] P37: Very Low Food Security, Other, Female, Age 66, 3-person household

[168] P45: Low Food Security, Hispanic, Female, Age 30, 2-person household

[169] P50: Low Food Security, Hispanic, Female, Age 22, 3-person household

You should be strict on trying not to make our children obese and sick, you know? Childhood diabetes is not a joke. And these children are having heart attacks and strokes. And it's just, that's, that's crazy. I just, I just think you should, they need, a lot of people need help. They need to learn how to [eat right]."[170]

Another offered similar recommendations: "Yeah. More helpful if they created a way that would teach people how to make their dollar go further because the reality is they're never going to stop the Food Stamp program. If you're going to have the program, why don't you teach people how to make those dollars last?"[171]

Two respondents had interesting, outside-the-box ideas about how to improve SNAP. One respondent talked about possibly having coupons preloaded onto SNAP cards, both to save money and to encourage healthier eating.

"If Food Stamps came preloaded with some type of coupons that are loaded by the manufacturer for purchase...—coupons that already exist out there. Like with Sam's Club—you go into Sam's Club and you scan your card...it automatically prints out [coupons] based on your purchases, coupons for things you're likely to spend money on. Well, it would be simple for the USDA to do the same thing with manufacturers so that people can automatically save money on food that they're already purchasing."[172]

Another talked about the possibility of giving small SNAP bonuses near holidays like Christmas, when people need to buy more food.

"[They should] do more on the SNAP to maybe, like...give an extra $5.00 or $10.00 onto your SNAP. I would say like every three months, yeah every three months to or when it's close to the major holidays.... I mean, it would help [during] the biggest [holidays] and would be nice to give it at Christmas, when most people do the majority of cooking."[173]

H. Chapter VI Summary

SNAP recipients report varied experiences with SNAP, both in their interactions with SNAP offices and in the help SNAP gives them to maintain a constant supply of food in their household. Many say that, most importantly, SNAP benefits help relieve some of the pressure they feel to juggle their financial obligations while keeping enough food on the table. Families at all levels of food security told us that SNAP allowed them to purchase more food, and more healthy food than they would otherwise be able to "afford." This is because they must use their SNAP benefits for food; resources in this form cannot be traded off to meet other urgent financial needs. Given their often

---

[170] P38: Food Secure, Black Non-Hispanic, Female, Age 26, 3-person household

[171] P7: Very Low Food Security, White Non-Hispanic, Female, Age 41, 4-person household

[172] P7: Very Low Food Security, White Non-Hispanic, Female, Age 41, 4-person household

[173] P47: Food Secure, Black Non-Hispanic, Female, Age 33, 3-person household

precarious economic circumstances, many claimed they would not be able to eat in the absence of SNAP. Those who had recently lost SNAP benefits did often report that they skipped bills to cover their food needs, but they also skimped on food purchases, skipped meals, and sometimes even "starved"—went without any food for a day or more—as a result. A Chapter III showed, loss of SNAP benefits is a common trigger of food hardship, especially among the less food secure.

At the same time, respondents frequently asserted that their SNAP funds carry them through the first two to three weeks of the month, while the "end of the month" is spent scrambling to meet food needs; households do not tend to set aside cash resources to purchase food during that last week or so. A common perception among respondents is that food has gotten more expensive, and benefits have not kept pace. The cycle of bills, income, and benefits is strained by the volatility some find in their eligibility for the program; respondents who have been on the program for a longer period of time gave accounts of repeated and abrupt losses of benefits. These unpredictable changes in monthly budget calculations can greatly disrupt a family's ability to meet their food needs. Other frequent sources of frustration for respondents revolved around interactions with their local SNAP offices. Caseworkers' poor attitudes, the unyielding eligibility policies, and the interminable application lines all contributed to the nearly universal perception that the SNAP program and its employees lacked empathy and treated beneficiaries with condescension. These views contrasted quite dramatically with respondents' experiences with the WIC program, which was acclaimed for its provision of nutrition information and its focus on health outcomes instead of eligibility concerns only.

This page has been left blank for double-sided copying.

VII. IMPLICATIONS FOR FUTURE RESEARCH

The study's findings suggest several directions for future research.

Obtaining Detailed Information About Fluctuations in Household Expenses and Income

Although data is available about the income and expenditures of SNAP participants, detailed income and expenditure data are rarely collected in the same data set. Surveys tend to focus either on collecting complete, itemized income data or complete, itemized expenditure data. Furthermore, the data are often limited to cross-sectional data collected at a point in time.

For example, the SNAP Quality Control (SNAP QC) data, used to produce the annual "Characteristics of SNAP Households" reports published by FNS, contains complete information on SNAP participants' monthly incomes, but contains only limited expenditure data (medical, shelter, and dependent care expenses) and consists of repeated cross-sectional samples with different households interviewed throughout the year. The Survey of Income and Program Participation (SIPP) follows the same households over time and collects household income data for monthly reporting periods spanning several years, but it collects limited expenditure data that is typically on an annual basis. The Consumer Expenditure Survey (CE) collects detailed expenditure information and follows consumer units (households) over four quarters. However, it collects only limited income data.

The IDI findings related to the relationship between food insecurity and financial shortfalls suggest that there would be value in obtaining more detailed information about SNAP participants' expenditures and incomes just after entering the program and following them through the first few months. This would allow FNS to understand how households reallocate scarce income resources once they receive SNAP benefits to meet obligations such as rent, utilities, transportation, and other basic needs. In addition, expenditure information could be obtained according to what was owed versus what was paid in order to help explain how households reallocate income and the extent to which households "juggle" (keeping some creditors at bay while others' demands are satisfied). This research might reasonably consist of a combination of IDIs to obtain input from SNAP recipients, together with standard survey methods to obtain information about the actual fluctuations in circumstances that occur over time.

Exploring Family Networks as a Food Coping Strategy

We found that a significant minority of the food secure households in the study take advantage of frequent invitations to relatives' homes for meals and receive contributions of groceries and cash from their family and friends. Those who are less food secure were found to have less access to such resources. There would be value in obtaining more detailed information related to households' access to family networks and the role of family networks in alleviating food insecurity. The SNAPFS telephone survey collected a limited amount of information related to the *availability* of help from family, friends, and community members, but learning more about the extent to which households use these resources and how this use varies throughout the month is a fruitful area of research.

Food Access and Proactive Coping Strategies to Maintain Food Security

Many studies assessing food access limitations of low-income households have examined the availability of food by store type (supermarket, grocery store, convenience store, and so on), or even the quality of food (fresh produce versus canned or frozen goods) in the areas in which households live. More research is needed, however, on how households make food purchase decisions within this environment and how this relates to food security. In particular, more information is needed on households' proactive coping strategies such as carefully researching the best prices on particular products, traveling to multiple grocery stores several times a month to capitalize fully on sales, and carefully planning the meals around what is on sale rather than on the households' food preferences. We found that households who were the least food secure were also the least likely to engage in these strategies. Data would be used to explore the extent to which these strategies help to alleviate food insecurity.

Accuracy of SNAP Participant Perceptions of Food Prices at Different Stores at Which They Shop or to Which They Have Access

Many of the IDI respondents reported that they spend considerable time seeking out the best bargains for the food they buy. However, we know relatively little about how accurate their perceptions of relative prices are. It would be of considerable interest to conduct a study involving both in-depth interviewing and field work at a set of stores to determine the degree to which clients' perceptions of relative prices are correct. The results could shed light on whether additional program education activities could potentially help clients to spend their SNAP dollars more wisely.

The Relationship Between Physical and Mental Health in Needing SNAP

There is considerable evidence in our work that health issues, both mental and physical, may contribute substantially to patterns of SNAP use—both in determining patterns of entry and exit and also in altering the probability of long term use. However, relatively little is known about the incidence of such health-related factors in the SNAP population. Research to fill this gap could potentially involve a combination of closed-ended survey methods and also in-depth interviewing. In particular, the former could obtain detailed information about health histories over time, and the probing in the latter could obtain information on how respondents themselves believe that health factors have affected them and their participation in SNAP.

Planning for the End of the Month, when SNAP Benefits Typically Run Out

One of the most striking observations in the current research is how many households fail to budget money with which to buy food during the time at the "end of the month" when SNAP benefits typically run out. A key set of questions involves: Why not? Is this aspect of the program not communicated adequately to participants, or is it not relevant as households cannot do anything about it anyway? Is this an education issue – in other words, do SNAP recipients not know SNAP often is not supposed to cover food purchases for the whole month? What could the program do to change this disconnect between program users and design?

Exploring "Time Cost" as a Factor in Household Coping Strategies

Also, one of the particularly interesting findings is the "time cost" that families have in managing their food purchasing. Given the extensive nature of some families' strategies for cost-saving food purchasing, it would have been good to get a better sense of this time cost. Some respondents described efforts that seemed to be the equivalent of having a part-time job in terms of how time-consuming these strategies were, and it might have been worth asking about these time dynamics more systematically.

WIC Versus SNAP – What Works Best in One That Could be Applied to the Other?

Many of our respondents seemed to feel that WIC could serve as a "model" program and could potentially offer ideas for improving SNAP. This would suggest the usefulness of additional interviewing of households participating in both programs, in order to focus more directly on comparing them. Such detailed probing might also be able to shed additional light on reasons for various attitudes expressed and the degree to which those attitudes are experience-based.

For instance, a study might explore in more depth the tantalizing observation from our work that the respondents who felt that the substantial education component of WIC was good might not have been talking about themselves so much as their perception of the needs of other clients. A related potentially useful component of this potential study would be to examine the cost structure of the two programs. The point of this would be to determine whether any perceived advantages of WIC are due mainly to how the program operates or to how well funded it is on a per-client basis.

Improving SNAP

Related to the previous topic, it would also be useful to interview more clients on the issue of how SNAP can best meet their needs. To be sure, some of the things clients may discuss in such conversations may be issues beyond the control of FNS, such as the amounts of benefits or the use of income verification requirements. However, IDIs, if carefully focused, might be able to identify somewhat smaller changes in administrative practices which nevertheless would represent useful changes in making the program more accessible to potential clients

Reasons for Temporary Suspension of Benefits

Many respondents in our study indicated that temporary suspensions of benefits for a month or two (or even longer) often posed significant hardship for them and their families. Many thought that their own actions were not responsible for the suspensions, (although experienced case workers would be likely to argue that there is often "another side of the story" from the administrative office's point of view).

Building on the work FNS is currently doing related to churning, we believe that this issue could be significantly informed through detailed interviewing of recipients. However, in order to understand the whole picture it would be important for the researchers undertaking such a study to have access to selected hard copy and electronic case records and, to some extent, to the relevant caseworkers.

Such a project would examine whether a set of specific suspensions were the result of client error, office error, both, or neither. However to achieve its maximum usefulness, the study would also need to focus more broadly on the functional causes of the mistakes, rather than just the "blame." For instance, even in instances where the client was clearly responsible for having been late in submitting needed material, an important question to examine is whether there were simple changes in communication methods that could have totally prevented the problem.

This page has been left blank for double-sided copying.

REFERENCES

The American Association for Public Opinion Research. 2011. *Standard Definitions: Final Dispositions of Case Codes and Outcome Rates for Surveys. 7th edition.* AAPOR.

Boyd, Melody, Kathryn Edin, Susan Clampet-Lundquist, and Greg Duncan. "The Durability of Gains from the Gautreaux Two Residential Mobility Program: A Qualitative Analysis of Who Stays and Who Moves from Low-Poverty Neighborhoods. *Housing Policy Debate.* 20(1): 119-146. 2010.

Clampet-Lundquist, Susan, Kathryn Edin, Greg Duncan and Jeffrey Kling. "Moving Teenagers Out of High Risk Neighborhoods: How Girls Fare Better than Boys. *American Journal of Sociology.* 116(4): 1154-89. 2011.

Coleman-Jensen, Alisha, Mark Nord, Margaret Andrews, and Steven Carlson. Household Food Security in the United States in 2010. ERR-125, U.S. Dept. of Agriculture, Econ. Res. Serv. September 2011. available at http://www.ers.usda.gov/Publications/ERR125/ERR125.pdf

Edin, Kathryn and Laura Lein. Making Ends Meet: How Single Mothers Survive Welfare and Low-Wage Work. New York, NY: Russell Sage Foundation. 1997.

England, Paula and Kathryn Edin. Unmarried Couples with Children: The Unfolding Lives of New Unmarried Urban Parents. New York, NY: Russell Sage Foundation. 2007.

Mabli, James, Stephen Tordella, Laura Castner, Tom Godfrey, and Priscilla Foran. "Dynamics of Supplemental Nutrition Assistance Program Participation in the Mid-2000s." Final Report Submitted to the U.S. Department of Agriculture, Food and Nutrition Service, Washington DC, September 2011.

Mendenhall, Ruby, Kathryn Edin, Susan Crowley, Jennifer Sykes, Laura Tach, Katrin Kriz and Jeffrey R. Kling. "The Role of the Earned Income Tax Credit in the Budgets of Low-Income Families." *Social Service Review.* 2012.

Nord, Mark, and Gary Bickel. "Measuring Children's Food Security in U.S. Households, 1995-99". FANRR-25, USDA, Economic Research Service. 2002.

Nord, Mark and Anne Marie Golla. "Does SNAP Decrease Food Insecurity? Untangling the Self-Selection Effect," Economic Research Report 55955, Economic Research Service, USDA, Washington DC, October 2009.

Ratcliffe Caroline and Signe-Mary McKernan. "How much does SNAP reduce food insecurity?" The Urban Institute. March 2010.

Seefeldt, Kristin S. Working After Welfare: How Women Balance Jobs and Family in the Wake of Welfare Reform. Kalamazoo, MI:W.E. Upjohn Institute for Employment Research. 2008.

U.S. Department of Agriculture, Food and Nutrition Service, Office of Research and Analysis, Characteristics of Supplemental Nutrition Assistance Program Households: Fiscal Year 2010, by Esa Eslami, Kai Filion, and Mark Strayer. Project Officer, Jenny Genser. Alexandria, VA: 2011.

Yen, Steven T., Margaret Andrews, Zhuo Chen, and David .B. Eastwood. Food Stamp Program Participation and Food Insecurity: An Instrumental Variables Approach. *American Journal of Agricultural Economics* 90(1):117-132. 2008.

APPENDIX A

SNAP FOOD SECURITY IN- DEPTH INTERVIEW PROTOCOL

This page has been left blank for double-sided copying.

First I would like to thank you for taking the time to talk with me today. I really appreciate it.

[GIVE CONSENT FORM TO RESPONDENT]

As you just read in the consent form, I would like to ask some additional questions related to some of the issues covered in the earlier survey we did with you. Like the earlier survey, this one is sponsored by the U.S. Department of Agriculture which funds the SNAP program. The interview will take about 90 minutes, and your cooperation is completely voluntary. As a token of appreciation, we will be giving you $$$ when the interview is complete. Do you have any questions about the study or your participation in the study before we get started?

1. These days, a lot of people are struggling to make ends meet each month. Tell me, how is your family?

2. Let's talk specifically about your big monthly expenses. Let's take last month, for example. What were your five biggest expenses? ($$)

Now I'm going to ask you about bills a lot of ordinary Americans struggle with from time to time. (INTERVIEWER NOTE: You do not need to get specific dollar amounts for the items listed below, unless they are offered).

3. (Probe as to whether they have a housing subsidy, and what kind, or whether they are doubled up and paying less as a result). Tell me about the last time you had a hard time paying your rent/mortgage. (IF IN LAST 12 MONTHS) How did you cope?

4. How about utilities—heat, light, water and sewer? Tell me about the last time you struggled to pay your any of these bills. (IF IN LAST 12 MONTHS) How did you cope?

5. What about your cell phone/land line/cable/internet? Tell me about the last time you struggled to pay any of these bills. (IF IN LAST 12 MONTHS) How did you cope?

6. What about your credit payments? Tell me about the last time you struggled to meet these payments. (IF IN LAST 12 MONTHS) How did you cope?

7. What about other debts, like education loans or medical debt? Tell me about the last time you fell behind on these payments. (IF IN LAST 12 MONTHS) How did you cope?

8. What about child care? Tell me about the last time you struggle to meet those expenses? (IF IN LAST 12 MONTHS) How did you cope?

9. How about transportation? Tell me the last time paying for transportation was a challenge? (IF IN LAST 12 MONTHS) How did you cope?

10. What about medical insurance? (Probe for Medicaid, Medicare or SCHIP coverage) In your household, who is covered and who isn't? Tell me about the last time you struggled with how to pay for medical insurance? (IF IN LAST 12 MONTHS) How did you cope?

11. What about food? How much do you get from SNAP right now? How about over the last year? Are you receiving anything from WIC right now? How about over the last year?

12. Let's talk more about what you spend on food. Let's start with last month....(NAME MONTH). Take me through that month, starting with your biggest grocery shopping and what you spent. ($$)

13. Now let's talk about the other shopping trips you made last month. Let's talk about each of those. ($$)

14. What about each of the visits to the corner store to buy food last month. Let's talk about each of these. ($$)

15. So adding it all together, you spent about $XX on food shopping last month. Is that about right?

16. Okay, so adding it all together, your major expenses totaled about $XX last month, is that about right?

17. So tell me, how do you cover all these expenses? (GET $$ HERE WHEN POSSIBLE.)

18. A lot of people say there is a lot of month left at the end of the money.[174] How about for you? Over the last year, how have you coped during time where money was tight? Tell me all about the last time that happened? What about the time before that? How do you typically cope when the money gets tight?

(INTERVIEWER NOTE: Questions below about food hardship are especially sensitive to struggling families, who feel stigma in admitting that their children might have experienced food hardship. Thus, additional gentle probing might be necessary.)

19. We're especially interested in food. Tell me about the last time you ran short of what you needed to pay for food. How did you cope? How about the time before that? What do you typically do when the food budget gets tight?

20. People have all kinds of ways to make do when the food budget gets tight. Some skip meals. Others eat at a relative's house. Others go to food pantries or soup kitchens, that kind of thing. How about for you? (FOR EACH STRATEGY: Tell me all about that last time that happened.)

21. Some times of the year are easier on the food budget than others. For example, some families tell us it's a lot easier in months when their kids are getting free breakfast and

---

[174] This question is posed in an apparently leading way. This is intentional; families feel great stigma in admitting they can't meet all of their expenses. In the pilot test, families who could cover their bills with their expenses didn't seem hesitant to respond that that wasn't a problem for them.

Appendix A

lunch at school. Others say it's easier during the summer, when kids are off visiting relatives. How about for you?

22. For you, what are the toughest times to get by food-wise? How do you cope then? Tell me all about the last time that happened.

23. Other people say that the food budget gets tight when there are more mouths to feed than you thought there would be—relatives stopping by, or visiting for an extended period of time. How about for you? Tell me about the last time that happened? How did you cope? How do you typically cope with this kind of situation?

24. Sometimes, our strategies just aren't enough. Tell me all about the last time you ran out of food. How did you cope? Tell me the whole story from start to finish. What about the time before that? How did you cope? Tell me the whole story from start to finish.

25. Tell me about the last time you or someone in your household had to skip a meal because there wasn't enough food. Tell me the whole story from start to finish. What about the time before that? Tell me the whole story from start to finish.

26. Tell me about the last time you or someone in your household actually went hungry. Tell me the whole story from start to finish. What about the time before that?

27. Sometimes unexpected events can make it difficult to make ends meet and provide food for your family—an eviction or foreclosure, a job loss, a new baby, a divorce…even something small like a bunch of bank overdraft fees. Has something like that ever happened to you in the last few years? How did you cope? Tell me the whole story from start to finish.

28. So let's get even more specific. Think back to yesterday morning. Who ate breakfast at your house? What did they have? Tell me about anyone who had breakfast somewhere else, at school, ate out, etc.

29. Now what about lunch? Who ate lunch at your house? What did they have? Tell me about anyone who had lunch somewhere else, at school, ate out, packed a lunch, etc.

30. Who ate dinner at your house? What did they have? Tell me about anyone who had dinner somewhere else, ate out, etc.

31. Who cooked yesterday? Who was responsible for getting the food from the grocery store and planning the meals? Who paid for the groceries?

32. So how typical is yesterday of other days during the week/on the weekend (depending on whether yesterday was a weekday or a weekend). Tell me more about that (TMMAT).

33. Now let's talk about a typical day during the week/on the weekend.
(REPEAT QUESTIONS 29-33 ABOVE).

34. Now think back to all the special occasions you've celebrated over the last year....holidays, birthdays, etc. Who has hosted these celebrations? Who has cooked? Who has paid for the food? When you've had to cook or pay, how have you coped?

35. Now I'm going to use your imagination. Okay, typically you do your big shopping at what store? Alright, we've just arrived at that store. You are going to shop just the way you always shop—nothing fancy. Where do you head first. What do you buy. Where do you head after that? What's next? What's after that?

    Let's make sure we didn't miss anything.
    Fruits and Vegetables?
    Meats/Fish?
    Dairy?
    Cereals, pasta, beans, rice, other dry goods?
    The frozen section?
    Canned goods?
    Chips and soda?
    Other snacks?

36. On this imaginary trip, where you are shopping just like you usually shop, is there anything you want to buy that you just can't afford?

37. What do you buy that you think you shouldn't be buying?

38. In general, how do you decide what to buy and what not to buy?

39. What do you put in your cart that you find yourself taking out and putting back later? Tell me all about the last time that happened.

40. Where else besides Big Store X do you shop? What do you buy there? Take me through that store, and tell me what you usually buy and what you usually don't buy and why.

41. Do you shop anywhere else? Take me through that other store, and tell me what you usually buy and what you usually don't buy and why.

42. Any other stores I've missed? Food you buy at the drug store, the dollar store, the farmer's market, and so on?

43. Families eat out or get carry out for all kinds of reasons—sometimes they need a break from cooking or have no time to cook, sometimes it's just a treat for the kids, sometimes there's no place to store your food or to cook, and sometimes it's just too hot to turn on the stove. What about for you?

44. Tell me about the last time anyone in your household ate out. What about the time before that?

45. Let's think back over last month, XX (NAME MONTH). Tell me about all of the times each member of your household ate out? Who paid each time? When you paid, what did

you spend? So adding it all up, you spent about XX eating out last month. Is that about right?

46. Tell me how you first learned about SNAP? TMMAT. When did you first apply? Tell me the whole story of that experience from start to finish. What has been your experience with the program since then? Tell me the whole story from start to finish. What do you like best about SNAP? What do you like least?

47. Now think back to when you didn't get SNAP. Was your budget situation the same, better, worse? TMMAT. Was your food situation the same, better, worse? TMMAT.

48. What about WIC? Tell me how you first learned about WIC. TMMAT. When did you first apply? Tell me the whole story of that experience from start to finish. What has been your experience with the program since then? Tell me the whole story from start to finish. What do you like best about WIC? What do you like least?

49. What about other food programs you are part of. Tell me now you first learned about XX. When did you first start getting food from that program? What has been your experience with the program since then? What do you like best about that program? What do you like the least?

50. What do they tell you at the SNAP office about what foods to eat and so on? What do they tell you at the WIC office? What other places tell you about food and nutrition (ex. Head Start, a pediatrician). TMMAT.

51. How do you pay for food when you don't/can't use SNAP or WIC. TMMAT

52. A lot of families these days are coping by doubling up. A lot of other families are helping out by offering struggling friends and families a place to stay for a while. Sometimes people just stay for a few nights, sometimes it's a permanent thing, and sometimes it's somewhere in between. What about for you?

53. When people come in and out of the household, it can pose real challenges. Who pays what bills, who cooks, who eats what food, and so on. Issues around food can be particularly challenging. How about for you?
    a. For example, sometimes people stay in the household, but eat elsewhere. How about for you? Tell me about the last time you faced challenges over who would eat where.
    b. Other times, people stay in the household, but pay for and keep their food separately. How about for you? Tell me about the last time you faced challenges in this area.
    c. Other times, people stay in the household, and everyone eats together. How about for you? In this situation, who pays for what? Tell me about the last time you faced challenges over who would eat where.
    d. And other times, people eat in the household but don't stay there. How about for you? In this situation, who pays for what? Tell me about the last time you faced challenges in this area.

54. Sometimes within a household, some people are eligible for SNAP, WIC, other programs, while others are not. How about for you? How does that affect how your household handles food?

55. Some households face special issues related to food: food related allergies, for example. How about for you? Tell me more about that (TMMAT). How does that affect your monthly food budget?

56. How would you describe your health? TMMAT. What about the other members of the household? TMMAT.

57. Describe the most recent heath problem you've faced. TMMAT. What about other members of the household? TMMAT.

58. When was the last time you went to the doctor. TMMAT. What about other members of the household? TMMAT.

59. Which of your health problems are related to diet? TMMAT. What about other members of the household? TMMAT.

60. People have a lot of different ideas about what healthy eating means for them. What about for you?

61. Most families have both healthy and unhealthy habits. What are your family's healthiest habits? What are your family's most unhealthy habits? What prevents you from having more healthy habits? TMMAT.

62. If you could afford to purchase the food you really wanted, how would your eating habits change? TMMAT.

63. Some parents tell us that they want to feed their kids healthier foods, but their kids refuse what's given to them. How about for you? TMMAT.

64. Now let's talk more generally about your expenses. Expenses vary a lot from month to month. It's spring/summer/winter/fall right now. What bills go up and down depending on the season? (Probe for specific amounts. Probe for increases during the winter due to Christmas shopping and heating bills (if cold climate) and increases in food expenses during the summer due to kids being out of school.)

65. Now let's talk about how you cover these expenses. Tell me about all the resources—big and small—that came into the household last month. (Probe for exact MONTHLY amounts. A month=4.33 weeks. Probe not only for formal income, but also financial help from family and friends and "under the table" jobs. Probe also for contributions from others such as teenage children, fathers of children, etc.).

66. Income varies a lot from month to month too. Tell me all of the ways your household income has varied over the past year.
    a. Some people are only able to work some months during the year. How about you?

b. Some people say some months their baby's fathers help them out, while other months the well is dry. How about you?

c. Some people say their household income varies a lot month to month because different family members move in and out of the household. Did this happen to you?

d. Some people say they experience some kind of event that affects their household income. Has this ever happened to you? Something like divorce, a medical issue, that kind of thing?

67. These days, some people find they have to survive without any income from a job. How about for you? (IF YES) TMMAT. When was the last time that happened? How did you cope? Tell me the whole story from start to finish. What about the time before that? How did you cope? Tell me the whole story from start to finish. In the past year, how have you usually coped with this situation?

68. When your income falls short of your expenses, what do you do? Tell me more about that. Tell us all about the last time that happened. Tell me the whole story from start to finish. Tell me about the time before that. Tell me the whole story from start to finish.

69. When your income falls short of your expenses, how do you prioritize things and how do you decide what to pay first, second, and so on? Think about the following expenses and tell me how you prioritize them:

70. In the last year, what hardships has your household faced as you've struggled to make ends meet? Tell me about how you coped with these hardships.

71. For some people, there is a big windfall at tax time, because they get lots of tax credits. How about for you? TMMAT. How did you spend the money and how did you decide what to spend it on?

72. What do you think can/should be done to help your family makes ends meet in these tough economic times?

73. What do you think can/should be done to help families struggling to feed their families?

This page has been left blank for double-sided copying.

APPENDIX B

LESSONS LEARNED IN CONDUCTING SNAPFS IN- DEPTH INTERVIEWS

This page has been left blank for double-sided copying.

Our experiences in designing and conducting the IDIs provide useful information on conducting qualitative studies of the SNAP population. Here we describe some key "lessons learned," focusing on important tradeoffs between controlling project cost, maximizing response rates, making the sample as geographically representative as possible given the size of the sample, and the necessary qualifications for the field interviewers.

Usefulness of Using Randomization Methods to Maximize Geographical Diversity

Although the specifications for this qualitative study did not require formal statistical geographical representativeness of the SNAP households interviewed, we believed the study would benefit from interviewing households in different parts of the country. We selected States in which to conduct in-depth interviews from the set of 30 States participating in the SNAPFS telephone survey. The method we used was designed (1) to achieve a higher degree of geographic representativeness than we would through a random selection from the 30 States, and (2) to produce enough household respondents from the telephone survey to obtain 90 in-depth interviews.[175] The four locations chosen were Boston, Massachusetts; Houston, Texas; Indianapolis, Indiana; and Riverside, California. We believe that these methods contributed substantially to both the substantive findings and the face validity of the data collection and analysis.

Importance of Back Up Plans for Ensuring Adequate Sample

Sample size was a particular concern, because in-depth interviews were conducted only with households with children, rather than the full baseline sample. Furthermore, for reasons discussed in detail in Chapter II of the main Final Report of the SNAPFS study, the numbers of baseline interviews in the main survey proved to be somewhat lower than expected. These factors led to an initial shortfall in the original IDI sample, requiring the development of back-up plans to generate additional sample. For each of the four IDI study sites originally chosen (see above) we added additional sample from nearby urban areas that were also included in the main survey.

For instance, after beginning respondent recruiting in Boston, we realized that there were fewer baseline households with children in our survey sample than we anticipated that lived in the Boston area that could do the interview during the specified study period. In addition, the number of "no-shows", or households that said they would be home at the scheduled interview time, but were not, was greater than anticipated. For these reasons, we needed to expand the geographic area to meet the sample size target, and we did so by adding respondents from Rhode Island.

Looking back, selecting two cities, rather than a single city, in each of the four Census regions may have made it easier to achieve the targeted number of completed interviews. The travel costs would have been more expensive, but this might have been partly offset by lower respondent recruitment costs.

Costs associated with requesting approval from states to conduct these additional interviews would probably not have been a major factor. We successfully obtained approval from the relevant states to conduct the IDIs, in addition to the baseline and follow up interviews for the telephone

---

[175] The details of the sampling methods are described in Chapter I.

survey, and in general states expressed little concern about agreeing to our conducting the IDI work in addition to the main interviewing

Interviewing Venues

The interviews usually took place in the respondents' homes. On occasion, at the request of the respondent, they were scheduled in a public place such as a restaurant, library, or community center.

Conducting the interviews in the homes was valuable in that it allowed interviewers to include an observational component and record information about the home environment and the neighborhood. Additionally, being in the home environment generated important lines of inquiry. For example, observing a grandmother in the home allowed us to have a conversation about the importance of family networks as a coping strategy. Similarly, observing a SNAP household in a residence that lacked a full kitchen shaped a conversation about the challenges to maintaining food security. In another home, we observed stacks of canned soup that we learned served as a coping strategy during the last week or two of the month once SNAP benefits ran out. Being able to get tours of respondent's cupboards and refrigerators, seeing their stockpiles of food, and having respondents show us the coupons they use for food were useful strategies and led to more richly detailed data.

There were several operational and logistical challenges to conducting interviews in the respondent's home, however. These affected project schedule and cost. In general, our IDI interviewing staff were recruited centrally and were either Mathematica staff or associated with our lead consultant, Kathy Edin. At most locations, therefore, these interviewers were on "travel status" while doing the interviewing work. Conducting interviews in the respondents' homes often required interviewers to devote a full morning or full afternoon to a single respondent. Frequently, it took over an hour to travel to the respondent's home; the interview was, on average, about 90 minutes; and then it took an hour to return from the respondent's home. Because interviewers were in the field for a pre-specified amount of time (often about one week) and "no show" rates were quite high, it was costly in terms of time and resources when the respondent was not at home at the scheduled time. Finally, as with many household surveys, it was important to develop standard procedures that maximized the safety of the interviewers.

An alternative interviewing strategy would have been to conduct interviews in a centralized location such as a community center, to have multiple interviewers present, and to schedule respondents more closely together. This would have enabled us to better handle "no-shows" or cancellations, as the interviewer would have backup respondents readily available. To be sure, respondent transportations issues would have had to be addressed, but this could potentially have been done by providing respondents with transportation money for taxis or other transportation or by arranging for transportation to be provided by staff working for the project.

While we lack sufficient information to fully quantify these tradeoffs, we believe that further attention to this alternative model may be warranted. As a future area of methodological research, it would be interesting to compare the quality of the interviews conducted in public settings and the types of information we received to the interview quality and information received from conversations in respondents' homes.

Importance of Using Relatively Senior Research and Survey Staff As Interviewers

With a semi-structured conversation, qualified staff and excellent training were essential to ensuring the success of the data collection. While all interviewers gathered the same core content, the interviewers were authorized to change the order and wording of questions to suit the flow of the conversation.

In conducting the analysis and writing the report, we remarked at the high quality of the data. While we attribute this to several factors, we believe one that played an important role was the composition of the interview team. The interview team consisted of full-time Mathematica staff and Harvard University consultants with at least master's degrees who had experience working with low-income households and contextual knowledge of policies programs that may affect SNAP households. Because of the team's research experience, we were able to train the interviewers very quickly and thoroughly, which we discuss in more detail in the "In-Person Training Strategy" section below.

We also believe having interviewers play a lead role in data processing and data analysis helped to ensure consistency between data collection and analysis. As we discus in more detail in the "Coding and Analysis Process" section below, we had one experienced coder do all of the initial coding, which saved an enormous amount of time. Given that we had about 4,500 pages of data, training multiple coders and ensuring inter-coder reliability would have required a great deal more time and resources. Also, having one coder who was familiar with the universe of the data proved to be a helpful fact-checking resource during the analysis process. Additionally, including the interviewers in the analysis process also served as an important fact-checking mechanism.

Importance of Pre-Testing and Codebook Development

Senior researchers with previous experience conducting studies with low-income families about financial issues developed the interview guide. Writing the interview guide was an iterative process that included pre-testing the guide with a small sample of families who were not included in the formal study. Once the interview guide was drafted, it was field tested at a Headstart center in Boston, and six pre-test interviews were completed. One person conducted each of the interviews, while two people observed the interview. A representative from FNS was present at these interviews, and this was very helpful, since we were able to get feedback from the client about the kinds of questions that were being asked. Throughout the two day process of pre-testing, the interview guide was edited and reworked to reflect what we learned during these interviews. This included examining what questions worked well, what questions needed to be adjusted, and ways we could streamline the interview guide to make it as concise as possible while still getting as much detail as we needed. We focused especially on reworking the questions about food purchasing and consumption.

Two of the pre-test interviews were with Spanish-speaking interviewees, which allowed us to edit and improve the Spanish version of the interview guide.

Being Sensitive to Unexpected Themes

When writing an interview guide, tradeoffs have to be made about what areas to ask for specific details. As is the case with most qualitative studies, we found unexpected themes during data collection and analysis. One of the major findings from this study was how respondents are running budget deficits in a typical month. However, since this was not the primary focus of the study, the interview guide did not go into extremely specific detail about income and expenditures dynamics within households. When we conducted the coding and analysis we realized how important these budget dynamics were in families' lives, and because some families gave us more detail in this area than we asked about, we were able to code up complete budgets for about 60 percent of the sample. In retrospect, it would have been good to devote a bit more time to systematically capturing these details of families' overall budgets.

Also, one of the particularly interesting findings is the "time cost" that families have in managing their food purchasing. Given the extensive nature of some families' strategies for cost-saving food purchasing, it would have been good to get a better sense of this time cost. Some respondents described efforts that seemed to be the equivalent of having a part-time job in terms of how time-consuming these strategies were, and it might have been worth asking about these time dynamics more systematically.

In-Person Training Strategy

We were able to conduct a very thorough and efficient in-person training session with the interviewers in a short amount of time. The success of our training strategy hinged partly on the previously noted use of relatively senior researchers and analysts who were able to learn the interview protocol quickly. Additionally, we believe that the in-person, intensive training strategy we used maximized the effectiveness of the training. We did a two-day (half-day) training in which experienced qualitative interviewers trained the research staff on how to conduct in-depth interviews. We discussed the basic tenants of good interviewing skills, thoroughly reviewed the interview guide so the interviewers were familiar with the questions as well as the reasons we asked specific questions, and general guidelines about fieldwork. We then spent a significant amount of time role-playing interview situations, which we think was a really useful way to experience and observe a variety of interview interactions.

Coding and Analysis Process

The coding and analysis process was conducted in multiple steps. First, all of the transcripts were coded using broad coding categories that reflected the themes in the interviews. We used the interview guide to develop a codebook, and then pre-coded five interviews to see what additional themes emerged from the data. These additional themes were added to the codebook, which was then used to systematically code all of the interview transcripts. In order to avoid the issue of inter-coder reliability, we had one experienced qualitative coder do all of the coding. The data were coded in Atlas.ti, a qualitative software program. We think this process worked well, as it cut down immensely on the time and resources that would have been necessary to train multiple coders.

Once the primary coding was done, researchers each took a set of codes to do subcoding, or secondary coding. The larger thematic categories were analyzed for more specific themes. For example, one of the broad categories is "coping strategies." We then subcoded the data from the code into all the specific coping strategies that respondents utilized.

The researchers then wrote memos on each of the themes in the data, and from these memos we constructed the report. During the analysis process, the researchers had ongoing conversations with each other to ensure accuracy in the analysis process.

One area of the analytical process that we think could be improved in future studies would be additional training of the research staff in how to conduct analyses and write memos. We did the training for the analysis portion over the phone, given constraints in time and resources, but we think it would be beneficial to hold an in-person extensive training for researchers on the analytical coding and memo writing, and to workshop the steps in this process.

Qualitative Interviews Provide Very Useful Information about the SNAP Population

Incorporating a qualitative component into this project was extremely valuable. First, the qualitative interviews yielded rich, detailed data about a wide range of dynamics affecting the lives of families who participate in SNAP. Second, there were multiple themes that emerged from the qualitative interviews that we did not anticipate—typically a strong benefit of the qualitative research process. The more inductive process in qualitative data collection allowed us to learn relevant information that we would not have known to ask about in a more highly structured survey. Finally, our qualitative fieldwork developed additional questions that future research can address. In fact, there are ways that we see how even more qualitative data collection could further develop our knowledge of the experiences of SNAP participants. For example, repeat interviews and observations could help us further understand these dynamics, especially coping strategies.

www.ingramcontent.com/pod-product-compliance
Lightning Source LLC
Chambersburg PA
CBHW080303180526
45167CB00006B/2651